T0347395

Fighting Organized Crime in Southeast Europe

In recent years organized crime has become endemic in the countries of Southeast Europe, and in so doing it has become perhaps the greatest impediment to the development of the area. This book recognizes that we are now involved in an urgent debate into how to successfully tackle it. Drawing together leading academics in the field, this collection of essays makes a thorough and valuable contribution to the debate. The discussions range over national and regional policies, the West European dimension of the phenomenon, and the less often discussed role that the media and civil society can play in the battle against organized crime.

This is a special issue of the *Journal of Southeast European and Black Sea Studies*.

Ekavi Athanassopoulou is a Senior Research Fellow of the Hellenic Foundation for European and Foreign Policy, Athens.

Fighting Organized Crime in Southeast Europe

Ekavi Athanassopoulou

Routledge
Taylor & Francis Group
New York London

First published 2005 by Routledge
2 Park Square, Milton Park, Abingdon, Oxon, OX14 4RN

Simultaneously published in the USA and Canada
by Routledge
270 Madison Ave, New York, NY 10016

Routledge is an imprint of the Taylor & Francis Group

British Library Cataloguing in Publication Data
A catalogue record for this book is available from the British Library

Library of Congress Cataloging in Publication Data

ISBN 978-0-4153-4801-0

Contents

DOCUMENTATION

ELIAMEP'S FORUM ON NEW SECURITY ISSUES (FONSI):
'SHARED INTERESTS & VALUES BETWEEN SOUTHEASTERN
EUROPE & THE TRANSATLANTIC COMMUNITY'

Biographical Notes

Ekavi Athanassopoulou is Senior Research Fellow at ELIAMEP and Academic Director of ELIAMEP's project forum on New Security Issues: Shared Interests and Values Between Southeastern Europe and the Transantlantic Community, which focuses on organized crime and its interelated activities. Recently (2003) she was Visiting Fellow at the Pacific Council on International Policy, USA. She is the author of *Turkey: Anglo-American Security Interests 1945–1952: The First Enlargement of NATO* (1999).

Saso Georgievski is a Professor at the University Cyril and Methodius, Law School, Skopje, Macedonia.

Misha Glenny, during the Yugoslav crisis of the early 1990s, was the Central Europe correspondent for the BBC World Service. He is the author of a number of books, including *The Rebirth of History: Eastern Europe in the Age of Democracy*, and *The Fall of Yugoslavia: The Third Balkan War* (1992), *The Balkans* (1999). He is currently working as a political consultant on southeast Europe and divides his time between London, Brighton and the region.

Aleksandar Fatić is a Research Professor of International Relations at the Institute of International Politics and Economics in Belgrade. He directs the Security Policy Group of the Management Centre, a think-tank based in Belgrade. He is the author of numerous publications, including *Crime and Social Control in Central-Eastern Europe* (1997).

Radoslava Stefanova is officer at NATO's Political Affairs and Security Policy Division. Prior to her current employment she taught International and Transatlantic Relations at the American Universty of Rome and was Research Fellow at *Istituto Affari Internazionali* (IAI), Rome.

Ahmet İçduygu, is Associate Professor at the Department of International Relations, Koç University, Sariyer, Istanbul, Turkey.

Krassen Stanchev is one of the founders and Executive Director of the Institute for Market Economics (IME). He served as a member of the Constitutional Assembly of Bulgaria (1990–1991) and was founder of different civic groups and initiatives, among them the first private university, the New Bulgarian University. In 1996 he was named 'Best Country Individual Analyst' by EuroMoney. In 1995, he was one of the initiators of the Balkan Network (⟨http://www.balkannetwork.org⟩), a group that devoted resources and efforts to study economic peculiarities of the region.

Plamen Ralchev is a policy analyst at the Institute for Regional and International Studies. He has been a visiting fellow with the East Europe Program at the Center for Strategic and International Studies in Washington DC, and a guest lecturer at the National Security and Defence Department at 'Georgi Rakovski' Defence and Staff College, Sofia.

Emi Velkova is a Visiting Scholar at Boston University School of Law.

Susan Woodward is Professor of Political Science at the Graduate Center of the City University of New York. She is the author of *Balkan Tragedy: Chaos and Dissolution after the Cold War* (1995), *Socialist Unemployment: The Political Economy of Yugoslavia, 1945–1990* (1995) and numerous articles on southeast Europe, post-communist transition, state-building and crisis management.

Preface

This special issue on *Fighting Organized Crime in Southeast Europe* is the direct product of ELIAMEP's project, Forum on New Security Issues (FONSI): Shared Interests and Values Between Southeast Europe (SEE) and the Transatlantic Community. In the summer of 2002 ELIAMEP launched this project with the generous support of the German Marshall Fund of the United States. The initiative for this project derived from the understanding that organized crime – and its interelated activities – has emerged as the most serious security issue in southeast Europe, undermining stability and the rule of law – both essential for the gradual integration of the region with the transatlantic community.

Within the framework of this project ELIAMEP organizes two workshops a year, seeking thus to establish a regular forum for dialogue and for building mutual understanding and a consensus of approach between influential actors from the United States, the EU and southeast Europe regarding organized crime, terrorism and other non-traditional, interrelated security challenges in the region.

This volume contains papers presented at FONSI's workshops, papers on subjects discussed at the workshops and the executive summaries of the conclusions and recommendations reached by the 2003 workshops. With this publication ELIAMEP hopes that its project has an impact on a even wider audience and that it directly contributes to the academic debate on how to effectively fight organized crime in southeast Europe.

Ekavi Athanassopoulou

Fighting Organized Crime in SEE

EKAVI ATHANASSOPOULOU

The subject of organized crime is enormous. It has been called the new communism, the new monolithic threat.[1] Through violence and corruption it penetrates like a fast-spreading virus the legal economy and corrodes the regulatory apparatus. Its spread diverts resources away from the formal economy, undermines the central power essential to make the system work; it destroys the spirit of social collectivism. Controlling it depends as much on the resistance of social values and on a healthy economic environment as it does on policing and law enforcement. In geographical extension it neither starts nor ends in southeast Europe (SEE). Nonetheless the region is more than just another link in the chain of global crime; it has become an important bridge in criminal networks spanning from western Europe to Asia and Africa.

Since the 1990s SEE has emerged as the major gateway to Europe for the smuggling of thousand of illegal immigrants from the Middle East, Asia and Africa as well as for the trafficking of women and girls from the area and the former Soviet Union for the sex industry. It has also become a linchpin in the European cigarette-smuggling business and the bridge in the drugs route from Central Asia and Midlle East to western Europe.

In the context of the transition of the countries in SEE to market economies, stable democratic institutions and the rule of law, organized crime and the corruption it generates have been identified as the most serious obstacles to legal, political and economic reform.

In the last 14 years organized criminal enterprises have become established in SEE countries via the development of a strong criminal infrastructure supported by criminal groups and patronized through corruption by ruling elites. Often enough the criminal edifice has been

---

[1] By the American senator John Kerry (D-Ma)

kept in place with the aid of state institutions. The result is the creation of autonomous power structures which operate with imputiny from prosecution, extort payment from legally operating businesses, manipulate the starved-for-funds media and control political parties. These structures which are exemplars of multi-ethnic collaboration have also the capacity, we now understand, to disturb peace and sow the seeds of ethnic conflict in order to secure the environment within which they operate. Most alarmingly their thriving has been possible because of toleration and cynicism, in the best of cases, but also active involvement by a significant part of the public under the pressures of severe unemployment and minimal prospects for future employment opportunities. Thus the distressing possibility that a number of countries in SEE, instead of becoming integrated with the rest of Europe, will become permanent pariahs in the European system with their criminal organisations feed into world-wide criminal activities and the tide of terrorism which lives on them, is a very real one.

In the last five years regional governments, under increasing pressure from the international community and with an eye to having their countries accepted as members of the European Union, have been making a greater effort than ever before to break the back of organized crime in their territory. Transnational and international cooperation on border control has increased; the right pieces of legislation have been enacted; better coordination between the government and various law-enforcement bodies has been sought. This is a beginning; we still have to wait for concrete and permanent results.

The criminalization of politics in most SEE countries is so profound that it leaves little room for great optimism. Breaking the control structures that crime has built in these countries since the early 1990s and changing the kind of mentality that goes with them is a huge challenge. It demands unfailing commitment on the part of regional governments, but also crime-control initiatives that go beyond imposing supply-side solutions on demand-driven problems. Organized crime is market-based crime and never in history has an illegal market been defeated from the supply side. Indeed the essential message of most of the essays in this volume is that policing may be essential to fight organized crime in SEE but cannot solve the problem alone.

This collection makes no pretence at a comprehensive survey of the varied aspects of the battle against organized crime in SEE. Rather it concerns itself with certain understudied themes within the context of this battle, seeking to make a contribution to the debate on how to 'win the war' against organized crime in SEE. It is hoped that it will also help readers interested in contemporary SEE understand something of this big challenge facing individual countries in the area as well as the region as a whole.

The first chapter, by Suzan Woodward, focuses on the need for systematic conceptual analysis as a prerequisite in the fight against organized crime. Woodward underlines an essential but largely unnoticed problem: the agenda of the battle against organized crime in SEE gives the impression of being driven by politics and policy, not by knowledge and research results. In other words, it is devoid of a conceptualization of the deeper causes of crime and the wider effects of policy choises, without which a proper policy and public debate cannot develop. Woodward shows that a lot of the assumptions, upon which policies against organized crime in SEE rest, are problematic and makes the case for a specialist community which can 'establish standards of proof, identify causality, and promote priorities based on a set of shared normative and principled beliefs'.

In the following chapter Krassev Stanchev offers an interesting review of the economic – formal and informal – background to the rise of organized crime in SEE. He reminds us that in the 1990s all Balkan countries failed to follow policies which might have promoted sustained economic growth and prosperity. Even when growth was experienced for certain periods 'it was insufficient to compensate for previous periods of decline and deconstruction'. Thus for some time now most countries in the area have been characterized by chronic malfunctioning of the economic system and artificially generated employment which guarantees only extremely low salaries and sizable fiscal deficits. Given such an unhealthy economic environment in the SEE countries and the lack of serious prospects for economic growth soon, the author predicts that illegal economic activities will continue to offer the way out of poverty. In other words, organized crime in SEE is there to stay for some time.

Stanchev's conclusion does not mean that governments in SEE and the international community should consider the battle against organized crime futile. What it reminds us of is that organized crime is very different from predatory crime (robbery, fraud, etc.). There is a very broad social consensus that predatory crime acts, through which wealth is passed from one person or a group of person to another by use of force or fraud, are wrong. However, organized crime offences, particularly when they are related to a weak economic environment, involve mutually acceptable exchanges between criminals and a large segment of the population. Thus the social consensus against organized crime is much weaker if it exists at all. Therefore crime control initiatives need to move away from the cops and robbers, crooks and victims mind-set and address a whole range of problems including the basic question of how to stop poverty.

Misha Glenny's essay moves the debate right into the heart of public economic policy by touching upon perhaps one of the most sensitive issues in western Europe today: migration policies and more specifically access of the SEE labour force to the western European market. The essential message here is that organized crime in SEE has thrived against high rates of unemployment and stagnant economies. While the peoples of SEE are in dire need of employment the EU urgently needs to rejuvenate its labour force. However, only a tiny perecentage of immigrant visas are given to SEE citizens. 'In general, the EU has confirmed or in some cases made harder access to the EU for Balkan citizens.' 'The relationship between unemployment and organised crime in South Eastern Europe has not yet crossed into the discourse over visas and the labour market' in the EU. It will not be easy for Brussels to move in the direction of easing visa requirements for the labour force from SEE. Nonetheless, some creative thinking can go a long way towards benefiting both sides: for instance short-term contracts for seasonal workers from SEE. While long-term solutions to organized crime can only be found through systematic policies the importance of such steps is enormous.

The next four essays concern themselves with currently hot topics: organized crime in Kosovo and the institutional preparedness of the UN interim administration in the province (UNMIK) to fight against it; transborder human smuggling and trafficking between Turkey and Greece; customs corruption in SEE; and the anti-organized crime and anti-corruption efforts in Serbia.

Radoslava Stefanova's essay, the product of field work in Kosovo, the notorious criminal capital of SEE, gives us new insights into the extensive web of criminal activities there, their regional connections and the institutional battle against them. The unique position that the international community has in Kosovo has produced results but not the successes one would expect and hope for. What clearly emerges from Stefanova's research is that unless serious legal gaps are addressed and the links between organized crime and politics are broken UNMIK's fight against the well-established criminal networks in the province will be wrong-footed.

Human smuggling and human trafficking from Turkey to Greece (one of the eastern gates to Europe) has been a new thorn in Turkish–Greek relations for almost a decade although it never receives the international spotlight which is reserved for more longstanding problems between the two countries in the Aegean. Icduygu's examination of this important but neglected issue provides interesting information about the human smuggling business and the nascent Turkish–Greek cooperation against organized crime. His research highlights the complexity of human smuggling operations which often are individual-run operations and contrary to general belief are not conducted within the framework of a wide, centralized criminal organization. Under-standing this complexity, the author argues, is essential for control policies to yield proper results.

Fighting customs corruption in SEE is the subject of the next essay by Emi Velkova and Saso Georgievski. Clearly the serious links between corruption and organized crime in SEE are to be found in higher places than the offices of customs and borders officials. Nonetheless, it is obvious that rooting out corruption in customs is an essential step in the direction of controlling transborder crime. The authors look into the successful anti-corruption in customs reforms in central and east-ern Europe (CEE) and suggest that the CEE experience might provide some solutions for the reform of customs in SEE given certain similari-ties between CEE and SEE countries.

Aleksandar Fatić switches the spotlight on Serbia, where organized crime and corruption were recently identified as enemy no. 1 to the security and prosperity of the country. The author offers a good account of the efforts of the government in Serbia since the 'democratic revolution' of 2000 to improve criminal justice legislation and generally reform the public administration system in order to strengthen it in the fight against crime and corruption. The conclusion is that, although important measures have been taken, the effort has not been as system-atic or coordinated as it should be. Many reasons account for this, the reaction of vested interests to reform being one of them. While it is clearly up to the society of Serbia to make sure that reforms are pushed forward the author points out that the impementation of reform poli-cies depends a lot on international financial assistance as Serbia lives currently on foreign aid.

Finally, Plamen Ranchev looks at non-governmental organisations in SEE and their pivotal role in fighting organized crime and corrup-tion by raising public awareness and contributing to an informed public debate. As he points out, although civil society in SEE is still not mature, a growing number of NGOs in the area have identified the battle against corruption, a relatively new priority in public agenda, as one of their interests. 'This involvement is facilitated by the fact that anti-corruption projects increasingly attract the attention of potential Western donor organizations'. When it comes to fighting organized crime, so far civil society in SEE has been met with its own limita-tions. Nonetheless, the NGO's contribution in terms of analytical research has to be noted.

As this volume is put together, events unfolding in SEE are constantly changing the parameters around which the battle against organized crime is being fought. The biggest challenge in this battle is to outsmart sophisticated criminals by being ahead of them rather than always trying to play catch up. Therefore it is important that policy-makers in the region and the EU are constantly aware of the multiplicity of factors, both internal and external to SEE, which facilitate the growth and spread of organised crime. To this end we hope firstly that researchers of diverse disciplines will continue to look into these factors to help sharpen our knowledge and understanding. Secondly, that academic research will seek to be in close tune with policy makers in the EU and their priorities in the fight against organised crime both at home and in SEE in order to have a major practical impact. In the final analysis pressure on SEE governments to enact and enforce the legal and institutional reforms to assist the curbing of organised crime has come from the international community and the EU in particular. Local governments have so far shown that they lack the political will and resolve to seriously commit themselves to that task at their own initiative.

REFERENCES

Centre for the Study of Democracy (2002): *Corruption, Trafficking and Institutional Reform: Prevention of Trans-Border Crime in Bulgaria (2001–2002)* (Sofia: Centre for the Study of Democracy).
Freedom House (2000): *Nations in Transit 1999–2000* ⟨http://www.freedomhouse.org⟩.
Golstock, R. (1993): 'Organized Crime and Corruption', *Corruption and Reform*, 7.
Hagan W. (1983): 'Organized Crime Continuum: A Further Specification of a New Conceptual Model', *Criminal Justice Review*, 2/1.
Naylor, R.T. (2002): *Wages of Crime: Black Markets, Illegal Finance, and the Underworld Economy* (Ithaca, NY: Cornell University Press).
Terzieff, Juliette et al., (2001): 'Former Warlords in the Balkans are Building an International Criminal Empire', *Newsweek,* 21 March.
Van Duyne, P.C. (1997): 'Organized Crime, Corruption and Power', *Crime, Law and Social Changes*, 26.
United States Institute of Peace, (2002): *Lawless Rule Versus Rule of Law in the Balkans*, Special Report 97 (Washington, DC: USIP).

Enhancing Cooperation against Transborder Crime in Southeast Europe: Is There an Emerging Epistemic Community?

SUSAN L. WOODWARD

It is now a full decade since the United Nations Development Programme proposed a new security agenda for the post-Cold War world. Human security, as the 1994 Human Development Report proclaimed, should replace the militarized, state-centric focus of the past. Security was not only about territory, borders and arms but, at bottom, must be about people and their ability to survive. At the same time, development actors and agencies must take insecurity and violent conflict seriously. In attempting to refocus policy and to link these two communities, security and development, the report emphasized the global and interconnected nature of security. Whether in the spread of disease, of refugees and migrants, of arms, of terrorists, or of illegal trafficking and organized crime, the consequences of insecurity, war and poverty in poor nations affect the security of those living in rich nations. Borders do not protect and secure. North and south, rich and poor, peaceful and war torn share common interests in security and the necessity of cooperation between them to manage these common threats.

If one's measure of significance in this new security agenda is organizational focus, then for southeast Europe transborder crime has few competitors. The number of new initiatives, activities and involved organizations focused on this policy issue in the past five years alone is astounding. A 2001 report on trafficking in persons listed 18 working in eastern Europe alone. Organizations directly involved in Europe include the Central European Initiative (CEI), the Organization for Security and Cooperation in Europe (OSCE), the European Commission, the European Union (EU) Council and its secretariat, the Council of Europe, Europol, Interpol, the Southeast European Cooperation Initiative (SECI), the Stability Pact and the Adriatic Sea Initiative. In southeast Europe specifically one can cite: the SECI Regional Centre for the Fight against Organized Crime in Bucharest, the Stability Pact initiative on Organized Crime (SPOC) created in Sofia on 5 October 2000, its Task Force on Trafficking in Human Beings, the OSCE roundtables on human trafficking such as one held in Belgrade, 19–20 April 2001, and subsequent activities of the Initiative Board created by it.

The problem, of course, is not new. Interpol itself was created by the 1904 International Agreement on the Suppression of Human Trafficking. More recent international and regional conventions providing legal and normative agreements include the Strasbourg Convention of 1990 and the UN Convention against Illegal Drug and Psycho-active Substances of 1988. But there does appear to be a significant escalation in attention to the problem in the past five years; for example, the International Convention against Transnational Organized Crime, created by the UN General Assembly on 9 December 1998, finalized at the 10th session of ad hoc meetings in July 2000 at Vienna, and signed at Palermo in December 2000, the two subsequent protocols to the Palermo Convention, the London Statement of the Lancaster House Ministerial Conference of 25 November 2002 on 'Defeating Organised Crime in South Eastern Europe', and the 'Statement on Commitments to Legalize the Status of Trafficked Persons' signed on 12 December 2002 by the ministers of interior of southeast Europe. The approach of the latter, refocusing on victim/ witness protection, was extended to child trafficking at a task force meeting in Slovenia on 28 March. Similarly, the Greek presidency of the EU (first half of 2003) gave priority to a follow-up of the London conference, including focus on an issue of longstanding concern to police in the region, an EU visa regime and a visa-free area or unified visa regime for the western Balkans, and made it one of the primary concerns of the Thessaloniki Summit on 21 June 2003 between the EU and countries of the Stabilization and Association Process (SAP). In addition, the Stability Pact, the SECI regional centre, and the University of Trento have an ongoing research project to improve and assess the functioning of information exchange in the fight against organized crime.

This brief and partial list does not even mention the myriad programmes of assistance to particular countries in the region, for example for training of border police and customs officials, on money laundering, on mechanisms to share intelligence between states in the region, to buy back weapons, and to harmonize official activities in this field.

Like the broader human security agenda, however, one gets the impression from the research side of this issue that this is an agenda driven by politics and policy, not by knowledge and research. While the grey literature – the policy documents, attempts to develop operational best practices and standard operating procedures, the field reports from humanitarian and peace-operation missions, and the UN agency studies – is huge, serious research is remarkably thin. It is also noticeably uncritical, characterized more by journalistic approaches, oft-repeated anecdotes, and dramatic summaries of dangers to persons and states without much conceptualization or empirical evidence on causes and effects of the kind one should expect. And while there may be emerging an epistemic community – 'networks of knowledge-based experts' (Haas 1992: 2) – on the issue of transborder organized crime, it does not appear yet to be taking an advocacy role for policy informed by that professional knowledge or even helping to frame the political agenda and public debate.

AN EPISTEMIC COMMUNITY ON THE ISSUE OF TRANSBORDER ORGANIZED CRIME IN SOUTHEAST EUROPE?

The growing influence of professional communities in international policy making and coordination that is asserted by international relations scholars is based on the 'growing technical uncertainties and complexities of problems of global concern' (Haas 1992: 1). The particular type of uncertainty that generates demand by policy makers for the information that these transnational communities of professionals can provide arises from the growing interdependence of individual states in their pursuit of policy goals on the policy choices that other states make. This uncertainty about the causal effects of particular policies taken by multiple actors is enhanced by the growing technical complexity of policy issues. In contrast to the more familiar focus on intentions and preferences, the advice sought from networks of specialists 'consists of depictions of social or physical processes, their interrelation with other processes, and the likely consequences of actions that require application of considerable scientific or technical expertise' (Haas 1992: 4).

To satisfy this need, such networks need not share origins, backgrounds or disciplines; they may include both academic researchers and practitioners, but they do share (1) a 'set of normative and principled beliefs', (2) 'causal beliefs' from their analysis of practices by which they can suggest 'multiple linkages between possible policy actions and desired outcomes, (3) 'notions of validity' and (4) 'a common policy enterprise' (Haas 1992: 3). Thus, they are joined in a common enterprise by specific knowledge, methodologies and normative values. Their authority with policy makers is based on 'their recognized expertise' in the particular policy domain. As a community, however, they may be quite informal, meeting at conferences, communicating through journals and generating joint research projects. Unlike traditional interest and advocacy groups, they are likely 'to engage in internal and often intense debates leading to a refinement of their ideas and the generation of a new consensus about the knowledge base' when faced with new information, discoveries or unexpected events in their issue area (Haas 1992: 18).

Nevertheless, the origin of the concept and of an associated explanation for policy influence lies with the fundamental sociological insight of knowledge as power. Whether intended or not, the activities of epistemic communities are political. They can shape public choices by helping policy makers identify state interests, framing the debate and alternatives for negotiation, and proposing the development of new social or political institutions. They are likely, as a result, to seek to institutionalize their influence with a more regularized pattern of cooperation and flow of information, by instituting monitoring activities, or even initiating proposals for enforcement. Whether they retain their original authority and goal of policy improvement, or move instead toward either a Gramscian role in buttressing existing power or a radical critique of current policy approaches and agendas, cannot be foreseen.

It is not yet clear whether there is an epistemic community on the issue of organized crime for southeast Europe. But the concept does help identify what its role could be should it emerge. It also helps identify the areas of shared interests, values, and consensus that would be needed. To assist the policy-making community, we would need to clarify our shared values, our methodological criteria of validity, a consensus on the state of our knowledge about cause and effect, for example, the causes of transborder organized crime in southeast Europe and the likely effects of specific policy choices, and our common interests in acting as a community. Such a discussion would necessarily extend to questions of representation – who belongs, who is not yet represented – and of forms of further cooperation.

To provoke that initial discussion about the bases of our current consensus and remaining disagreements, I propose three questions. First, is there a current approach to transborder organized crime in the region, can we agree on such a characterization, and is it well chosen? Second, what are the knowledge bases underlying the current policy approach, and do we agree with those assumptions? Third, do we have sufficient knowledge or do we need new knowledge, and if the latter, what kind?

THE CURRENT POLICY APPROACH TO TRANSBORDER ORGANIZED CRIME IN SOUTHEAST EUROPE

I propose that the current approach to this policy issue among those currently setting policy is a state-based approach that focuses on criminalization, defining a set of activities as crimes, and on developing the operational and technical aspects of implementing state agreements on such criminalization.

This approach is being channelled through the European integration process. Operationalization begins with legislation and institution-building defined by EU practices. States in southeast Europe are expected to meet what are called 'European standards' by adopting specified legislation and implementing institutions of law enforcement (police, judiciary) as part of the conditions for eventual EU membership. This approach is, therefore, characterized by standardization and conditionality. Were there no European integration process and promises of eventual membership, however, the states of southeast Europe would face the same standards and expectations from United Nations agencies and conventions.

Because of this approach, the key actors are domestic – legislatures, police, courts, intelligence services, ministries of the interior. Although many of the resulting legal and policy documents emphasize its economic aspects (both as cause and consequence), the relevant actors are security-sector officials, not economic or social policy officials. The approach is one often called 'securitization'. Transborder organized crime is seen as a security threat to be treated as such. Whatever ambivalence citizens in these countries may have about the illegitimacy and illegality of these activities and their participants for reasons of high unemployment and their own economic survival, they are expected to give the security threat higher priority and thus to accept the line drawn by the law and change their values accordingly. Because the networks of organized criminals cross borders and involve cooperation across those borders, moreover, these domestic agents are expected to cooperate, too, across borders. Regional cooperation (i.e., between states within southeast Europe) is a central plank in this new security agenda.

While there is no consensus on where the primary source of the problem lies – within southeast Europe or in the fact that the forces of both supply and demand lie outside the region – no one challenges the argument that transborder organized crime is by definition a regional and international issue, not a domestic one alone. Thus, cooperation must extend beyond the states within the region of southeast Europe to cooperation between individual states and the variety of regional and international organizations involved. Such cooperation emphasizes the sharing and exchange of information, joint operations, judicial networking, mutual legal assistance and, eventually, a common approach to the problem of transborder crime, as would follow from the 'standardization' goal.

Policy initiatives and priorities appear to be placed on types of trafficked (bought, transported, sold) goods: human beings (illegal migrants and asylum seekers, women and children primarily for the sex trade but also human organs, enslaved work, etc.), illegal drugs, weapons, and a catch-all 'major crime of other kinds' that is usually left vague, although contraband goods such as stolen vehicles, cigarettes and oil are often listed.

At the same time, discussions of organized crime are frequently linked with corruption, particularly the corruption of officials (both administrative and elective). The fight against corruption follows the same approach and thus policy often equates the fight against organized crime and against corruption, namely, the task is to classify corruption as crime, inculcate those values in the population so that they view such acts as illegal and subject to penalties, and focus on law enforcement, that is, on instituting financial controls and on policing (e.g., cut transborder networks through the interruption of financial links, confiscate proceeds of criminals and equally of officials within countries or in foreign banks, arrest criminals and corrupt officials).

Many aspects of this policy approach remain underdeveloped or contentious. There is, for example, substantial discussion about tactics, for example, the current concern with victim help and protection and discussions about how to raise public awareness on the assumption that public opinion and civil society associations are useful weapons in the fight. Another debate is whether cooperation is better effected on a functional basis (e.g., among customs officials, among police, among judges) or on the basis of national teams, and what form of cooperation is more effective – ad hoc, regularized, or even permanent commissions and task forces. These tactics, however, all follow from the assumption of criminalization and state-based cooperation.

THE ASSUMPTIONS OF THIS CURRENT APPROACH AND AN INVITATION TO CRITICAL ANALYSIS

This policy approach, if I have correctly characterized it, is based on a set of assumptions that may be seen as a set of empirical hypotheses for which an epistemic community would be able to provide knowledge, either in support of the assumption or against it. For example:

1. transborder organized crime is primarily a security threat and is best treated that way,
2. criminalization is the best approach,
3. state-based instruments will be the most effective,
4. countries have a shared interest in the problem (i.e., one that overrides national conflicts of interest or competition on the issue),
5. improved cooperation within southeast Europe should be a priority and will have positive effects,
6. improvements in technical and operational aspects (the implementation of existing agreements and legislation) should be the primary current focus,
7. increased control over finances (profits, networks, laundering) will work in the fight against organized crime, and
8. the priority of focus should be on human trafficking and, secondly, on illegal/illicit drugs.

In order to generate the critical analysis that a specialist community could bring to this issue area, I will raise questions about four of these assumptions: securitization, criminalization, state-based approaches, and regional cooperation and common interest. I will conclude this section by asking whose agenda this is and thus whose interests are currently driving policy in this area.

Securitization

Southeast Europe is far from being the only region in the world that is threatened by transborder organized crime and the focus of policy concern. The topic is, therefore, particularly susceptible to comparative research and the drawing of policy lessons from other areas. For example, the US 'war on drugs' and its policy focus toward Colombia in particular (as well as Mexico, Bolivia, Peru and others in South America), it is generally agreed, has not been productive, indeed has backfired. While the Taliban appears to have had some success with prohibitions against the production of poppy for heroin in Afghanistan, the aftermath of the military intervention in 2001 has been a skyrocketing renewal in poppy production by 2002–2003. Even if one shifts from military to policing methods, the fight against organized crime in American cities suggests modesty on causes and expectations of eradication. Even within a security focus, discussion as to tolerable limits and how such magnitudes and proportions should be measured – by quantities trafficked, amounts earned, proportion of economic activity engaged, persons employed, territorial spread, or social, economic or political consequences – would seem to an important part of the modesty recommended by global comparisons.

As with the US war on drugs, the EU focus on southeast Europe and the increasing attention by Justice and Home Affairs (JHA) arises from the threat of such trafficked goods (persons, drugs) into member countries of the EU. But to what extent is transborder organized crime also a security threat to states in southeast Europe? How do publics perceive it? To what extent is a policing, security-based approach most effective?

By focusing on crime and on transit, the EU (especially JHA), OSCE, UN and bilateral donors identify their partners in the fight on crime as ministries of interior, justice, foreign trade and customs. To the extent that there is a security element to the problem, however, people in southeast Europe tend to believe that the issue is a result instead of unsettled borders and the heightened barriers against transit (with the resulting incentives to smugglers and smuggling) that comes from continuing political uncertainty about national borders. Thus, the unsettled political status of Kosovo, the remaining uncertainty about the status of the border between Serbia and Montenegro and status of its state union, and continuing concern about northwest Macedonia and the 'Medellin of the Balkans', Preševo valley in Serbia, combined with the effects of two militarized international protectorates cutting through the heart of the region (Bosnia–Herzegovina and Kosovo) are seen as primary sources of trafficking that require resolution first, before one can hope to deal a blow to transborder crime. In the meantime, priority should be focused on better implementation by NATO-led military forces in Bosnia–Herzegovina and Kosovo (and the EU-led forces in Macedonia) of demilitarization agreements already negotiated.[1] In the interim as well is the proposal, and the urgency with which it is held by people in the region, for an EU visa regime and a unified visa regime or a visa-free western Balkans. Analysis of the political and practical implications of such a proposal would seem to be in order.

Francesco Strazzari analyses 'mafia' along three dimensions: first, as source of intimidation, that is, as a powerful means of extracting resources, which includes the threat of violence; second, as icon, that is, both the idea that mafia cannot be dealt with politically and the related tendency to associate organized crime with the historical path of state formation in western Europe and thus the assumption that it is these processes that are playing out now in southeastern Europe; and third, as safety net, that is, as a form of assistance and protection against economic shocks and other unpredictable events, particularly when states are weak and unstable and unable or unwilling to provide that protection. This is a particularly acute aspect of organized crime in southeast Europe currently because of the regime transition – dismantling of the socialist welfare state, the further cuts in public expenditures of social benefits and employment, and the rising level of poverty and of 'working poor' under conditions of monetary stabilization and economic stagnation.

The latter two dimensions – the nature of the state in the current moment and the issue of economic and social security – gain far more attention in the current research by scholars from southeast Europe than the security aspect. The interest of donors is the reverse. The experience of Krassen Stanchev is emblematic. In 1994–1997 he applied repeatedly on behalf of his Institute for Market Economics in Sofia in cooperation with other policy research groups for monies to research the phenomenon of organized crime itself from the EU, USAID and the equivalent Swiss, German and Canadian development agencies, without success. After the opening of the arms depots during the 1997 political crisis in Albania and uncontrolled haemorrhaging of arms and ammunition, donors became intensely interested in research on the subject, but only on the security aspects.

The social origins of criminal groups, indeed, tell far more about causes. They tend to be people in sports, war veterans (e.g., in Russia, from the Afghan war, or the 'young generals' in Bosnian Croat areas), and former members of the downsized security apparatuses (police, internal security, intelligence). They all, in other words, have marketable assets to adjust to unemployment or the collapse of state sponsorship by filling the need for private security and protection to persons, private businesses and rival criminal gangs when the state is unable to perform that crucial function because institutional change takes longer than most programs of economic reform allow.[2] There is a security aspect in the absence of state provision, but the primary cause is the strategy of economic and political transition and the resulting weakness of states. Yet the same proponents of this strategy of transition emphasize, in the area of organized crime, policies that require strong and effective states.

Training programmes, which are very extensive in the region, are designed, moreover, by police for police at police colleges, such as the modules funded by Norway on 'trafficking in human beings', 'irregular migration' and 'trafficking in drugs.' The police, themselves, are the first to volunteer that they are not the appropriate instruments to do many of the tasks necessary to the problem at hand, for example, to 'protect and assist victims' of human trafficking, assist rehabilitation and reintegration, and deal with the trauma and stigma of prostitution. Security personnel are not trained psychologists, social workers or medical doctors.

Criminalization

The external (UN and European organizational) demand for legislation and its effective implementation to criminalize certain behaviours can be analysed in terms of the systemic economic and political transition taking place in southeast Europe, that is, as part of the broader effort to implant a system of laws, institutions and values appropriate to competitive liberal democracy and a capitalist market economy on former socialist systems. That transition, however, is far from simple or straightforward, and the effectiveness of the policy approach toward organized crime and corruption will depend on understanding the interaction between its policies and that context. This is the subject of substantial and ongoing research and should, in this particular case, generate further questions for research and analysis.

To what extent is this external demand aimed at clarifying prohibitions of activities whose legal status was actually fuzzy in the previous (socialist) system (for example, prostitution was not legal, but not wanting to admit its existence under socialism, governments remained largely silent on the matter)? If so, improving the technical effectiveness of law enforcement agencies is a small part of the changes that need to take place. To what extent, instead, is this external demand defining activities as criminal that were previously considered acceptable, even beneficial, or at least tolerated? The parallel with the development of the criminal law in the early transition from feudal orders to capitalist systems, that is, from a system of reciprocal obligations between lord and peasant and use rights as a mechanism of welfare and survival for the latter to a system based on private property rights is worth contemplating for the radical ruptures in peoples' expectations and behaviours and systemic character of the changes that had to occur (see Hay 1975). If, as Vladimir Gligorov argued during the workshop, laws are introduced that generally contradict popular views of what is and is not legitimate activity, then the incentive to circumvent laws perceived to be 'bad laws' will have a more pervasive effect on the rule of law in general. And in such cases, decriminalization and liberalization may be the more effective tool. The 'stick' can 'create criminality' as much as eliminating it.

A further aspect of systemic transition concerns the redefinition of the state itself in the current period. To what extent is the liberalization process, constraining the legitimate scope of state behaviour and redrawing the accepted border between public and private matters, an obstacle to the strategy of criminalization? The new states are weak both in capacity and in the absence of a settled notion of its legitimate boundaries. What, for example, should be the respective realms of state regulation and freedom? To what extent are associated outcomes such as the reprivatization of violence, education and welfare a transitional phase where states lack institutional autonomy and a monopoly over those activities proper to modern states, and to what extent are these the result of a new definition of state scope?

The transition also involves changes in norms and values. Particularly instructive is the widespread discussion in Serbia in early 2003 about whether a more effective method toward human trafficking and prostitution would be legalization of the sex trade. Similar to the debate on illegal drugs, that legalizing certain use can reduce the elements of organized crime, violence and imprisonment (and its consequences) associated with criminalization, Serbian advocates argue that legalization, or at least decriminalization, would make it easier to address those elements that are genuinely dangerous in the sex trade – the transborder trafficking (and de facto enslavement) by criminal elements, for example (Stijak 2003). Human rights and women's groups advocating legalization belong to a more general trend in the EU (such as in Germany) that can be seen as the stage of 'European standards' to which they aspire. But officials in Serbia, who are responsible for implementing European requirements for a law enforcement regime against such activities, are justifying that approach on the grounds that Serbian 'culture' and 'traditions' are such that the public will not be receptive to legalization. In an environment so saturated with foreign assistance and requirements, from the conditionality of donor aid to the EU integration process and the multiple international protectorates, it is not surprising that the line between what locals are expected to do and what outsiders are permitted should become a subject of frequent commentary. The message being sent by the local discussion is that the clear perception of double standards is a substantial obstacle to the normative local change considered necessary by these programs.

The distinction between legal and illegal profits necessary to the financial instruments of this approach (investigations, control of money laundering, seizure of proceeds) also breaks down quickly when the easiest way to launder the money from criminal activities is to invest in legal activities – construction being most common. Because the current phase of economic reconstruction in southeast Europe (post-war reconstruction and infrastructural development in general), particularly that designed by the World Bank, is heavy on construction, the opportunities are unusually great. Moreover, in conditions where foreign private investors have been reluctant and scarce, any source of local investment is welcome and it is understandable if people look the other way. Indeed, foreign advisors place great stock in the diaspora and wealthy individuals as sources of investment capital in this phase but whose origins may not be scrutinized carefully. A particularly public case was the invitations to invest in a joint venture between Americans and rich Kosovars to build an American University of Kosovo, and the accompanying explanations to cover clear money laundering.[3]

Independently of the tasks of systemic transition, criminalization presumes that enforcement will act as a deterrent. Yet the academic literature is voluminous on the failure of a threat of punishment to deter in the face of growing poverty and economic hardship, on the one hand, and the huge profits that can be made for such activities, on the other.[4] Moreover, unlike common murder or theft, for example, the network character of organized crime makes the individual criminal unimportant, easily replaced if caught with new recruits. The size of the recruitment base in current economic conditions in southeast Europe is large enough to overwhelm law enforcement capacities. Comparison with the global war on terrorism since 11 September 2001, which has the same strategy (securitization, criminalization and instruments to control and limit financial gains) and has also not been successful, suggests that motives of the participants matter and may not always be vulnerable to the assumptions of this strategy. The links between criminal organizations and their support base requires research.

State-based

Perhaps the most radical criticism of the current approach comes from Moisés Naim, editor of Foreign Policy, in a recent article entitled 'The Five Wars of Globalization' (Naim 2003). After urging modesty because the illegal trade in drugs, arms, intellectual property, people and money and the wars by governments against them have been going on for centuries, he argues that governments can never win if they continue to fight them as 'enforcement problems' and by 'customs officials, police officers, lawyers, and judges'. This is increasingly true in current conditions. The tools are 'obsolete', the laws 'inadequate', the bureaucratic arrangements 'inefficient', and the strategies not directed at the methods of organization and resulting flexibility of criminal cartels. In particular, an approach that is based on 'repression', 'sovereignty', legal frameworks and law enforcement will fail. In southeast Europe, researchers argue that criminal gangs are the most modern in their technological skills and equipment, for example. The sums they can earn surpass by far the GNP of many of the countries in the region.

Naim's recommendations, however, for new mechanisms and institutions and a move from prohibition to regulation require returning to the case made by local scholars and officials in southeast Europe, that the primary focus should be on the development of effective states and the more complex capacities needed for regulation. The scope of this task is, of course, enormous if one takes into account the interdependence between legal politicians and illegal activities, as a result of connections established for war or opposition, of the search for monies to fund political parties, election campaigns, and the media, or as a result of everyday corruption.

Regional Cooperation and Common Interests

One of the primary criticisms of the current wars on illegal trade and its consequences levelled by Naim is the neglect of multilateral institutions for fighting such activities. As a truly global phenomenon that gains its flexibility from not being tied to territory or sovereignty, it is astonishing, he writes, that Interpol 'have a staff of 384, only 112 of whom are police, and an annual budget of $28 million, less than the price of some boats or planes used by drug traffickers'. Europol, similarly, 'has a staff of 240 and a budget of $51 million'.

In the case of southeast Europe, police professionals emphasize that while greater regional sharing of information and cooperation among professionals is very important to their task, the cooperation that is needed most is with countries further afield in the trafficking chain between supply and demand. For example, Albania needs to cooperate with Pakistan, Sri Lanka and Kurdish groups (especially Turkey), which are the sources of highly paid migration routes, and with Italy, which is the first port of trafficking in children and women. A successful example is the effective cooperation between the United States, Italy and Albania in interrupting a massive drug smuggling ring between Colombia and Albanian and Russian networks in 2001 to supply the west European market. The particularly important role of diasporas in creating long-distance networks, mobilizing and laundering funds and providing external sanctuary – critical to the cases of southeast Europe – also demonstrate the inadequacy of a focus on regional cooperation within southeast Europe alone. At the same time, territorially defined competition over trafficking routes in southeast Europe does introduce an element of national competition that interferes with such regional cooperation as well. As long as current economic conditions persist, this obstacle to effective implementation at the level of southeast Europe is likely to continue.[5]

Whose Agenda?

The London conference of November 2002 made it clear that the issue of organized crime in southeast Europe is now a matter of EU integration processes, and cooperation on this issue from countries in southeast Europe now a subject of conditionality – no cooperation, no progress on integration. To what extent is this agenda also a domestic one in southeast Europe? Whose interests are engaged?

The policy emphasis on technical and operational improvements assumes that political commitment is a settled matter – that the issue is not politically contentious within the country or among the political leadership. However, police officials insist that the problem of implementation is not a matter of legislation, conventions or bilateral agreements – all of which are now sufficient and some of which are even good, for example, the Palermo convention. The source of the problem is the absence of political instructions.[6]

To the extent that political commitment does exist, then a second obstacle is insufficient resources. Three aspects can be identified. First, the resources necessary to fulfil international commitments have not been forthcoming from donors. Activity setting standards and conditions has not been matched with the flow of funds.

Second, the effect of the attack by Al Qaeda on New York and Washington in September 2001 was to introduce a new American agenda to the problem of illegal trafficking and organized crime. While a substantial amount of EU activity and redefinition of NATO tasks have adjusted to American demands, there is a growing divide within the transatlantic community about priorities. This necessarily affects the amount and kind of resources available. For the EU states, priority remains on the transit of drugs (particularly heroin, 80 per cent of which moves along the Balkan route to western Europe) and illegal migration, and therefore the jurisdiction of Justice and Home Affairs. For the US, priority is the war on terror and the sharing of intelligence and tactics to interrupt networks and arrest and extradite potential terrorists who might use southeast Europe as sanctuary and organizing base but who could target the US. And for the UN and its related agencies, however, the new humanitarianism of the human security agenda remains strong so that trafficking in human beings (particularly women and children) and in light weapons retains priority. These conflicting priorities place resource-strapped countries of southeast

Europe in a difficult position politically, a position made worse by the conflicting foreign policy positions of the EU and the US on matters such as Iraq and the International Criminal Court.

Third, even if governments in southeast Europe are unambiguously committed to the fight on organized crime, both within their home territories and in transit across them, they must balance competing priorities of other policies. For example, the requirement of the market transition and economic reform (aimed at economic revival) is that public budgets be cut. When the World Bank requires Albania to cut 800 police to reduce its budget deficit, which commitment takes priority? Similarly, the external pressures of economic reform programs for states in southeast Europe to reduce their scope, particularly their regulatory power, and the demands to decentralize for both economic reform and conflict-management run counter to the findings of the academic literature on the policy measures best suited to fight corruption, namely, the importance of strong, effective states (particularly the 'centralization of rent-collection machinery' and the 'ability to pre-commit credibly')(Bardhan 1997: 1341).[7]

DO WE NEED MORE KNOWLEDGE? IF SO, WHAT QUESTIONS NEED ANSWERS?

Discussants at this workshop disagreed about the level of our knowledge and the need for more research on this topic. As one who felt the problem was not insufficient information expressed the problem, it's that 'everyone is involved' and the problem is 'how to prove it publicly'. If one reads journalistic accounts, interviews police officials and professional experts within police, intelligence, etc., offices or consults existing research on this topic, one is struck by how much we do know. But it is not systematic. And as police officials emphasize, the data do not meet the requirements necessary to win a case in court.

An additional obstacle lies, moreover, in the 'mafia as icon' phenomenon identified by Strazzari. On the one hand, organized crime is associated with danger, leading people to think it cannot be researched for fear of becoming victims of violence and intimidation themselves. On the other hand, the association of the phenomenon with political protection and collusion at the highest levels leads people to avoid investigations for fear of where it will lead, independently of the very real cases of direct intimidation. The best way to counteract this perceptual obstacle to research and public knowledge, Strazzari argues, is to demystify the issue by enlarging the community of researchers (international and transatlantic) who collect information on methods of organization, linkages and direct impacts on societies.

Epistemic communities provide antidotes to the secondary uncertainty generated for policy makers by complexity, whether arising from technical sophistication or interdependencies and spillovers among independent policy makers, states and issue areas. Their members establish standards of proof, identify causality, and promote priorities based on a set of shared normative and principled beliefs. To those ends, I propose a number of immediate research questions to generate debate and get the ball rolling.

First, is the data exchange system currently being created by the Transcrime project within the SPOC sufficient to the needs of the current regulatory system? If so, should it be communicated more widely; if not, what supplementary information is needed?

Second, do we have sufficient knowledge to distinguish among the three sources of organized crime in southeast Europe: those of transition, those that are structural, and those that are due to global flows beyond the borders of these states? For policy recommendations, these distinctions must be made. The three are also related, of course. To what extent, as Vesna Bojičić-Dželilović argues, have some transitional effects become structural and thus, in a negative feedback loop, interfere with further successful transition? For example, as she argues for Bosnia and Herzegovina in particular, to what extent have the effects of war become institutionalized in social dislocation, legitimation of criminal organizations, tight links between politics and smuggling, and the vast informal economy and in turn created a socioeconomic formation that is not conducive to democratization and economic reform and acts as an impediment to normalization of economic and political relations? Similar questions about the long-term consequences of the sanctions regime on Serbia, Montenegro, and Macedonia should be raised.

Third, what are public opinions regarding this subject? Do we know enough about citizens' views and the basis for their views to recommend adjustments in the current policy emphasis on mobilizing public support for action on such crime and relying to a great extent on civil society pressure and monitoring? Do the public distinguish, for example, between crime 'at source', crime 'in transit' and crime 'at its destination' as does the London Statement? Do citizens evaluate transborder crime differently from domestic activities of the same character and networks?

Fourth, would it matter to effective policy if there were more systematic research on and analysis of the social basis of recruits within southeast Europe? What causal linkages are implied?

Fifth, is there a territorial dimension to this problem such that a focus on particular states or unsettled borders, for example, would contribute to reduction? Is the problem an 'oversupply of borders' in general in Gligorov's terms or is it particular to specific places and times?

Sixth, do we have systematic studies of training programs to evaluate whether these imported programs are sufficiently sensitive to context to have good prospects for success?

Seventh, are the correct governmental policies being targeted, or should the focus be more on the tax and expenditure policies that currently create incentives to smuggling?

Eighth, in terms of the systemic consequences within southeast Europe, for example, on the kind of democratic politics possible or on future economic performance, can tolerable limits be identified? How would one define them and measure them; what should take priority?

ACKNOWLEDGEMENTS

I am indebted to colleagues who are specialists in this area and their willingness to share their knowledge generously over the past few years, in particular, Francesco Strazzari, Damjan Gjiknuri, Krassen Stanchev, Budimir Babović and Vesna Bojičić-Dželilović. An earlier version of this article was presented at ELIAMEP's workshop on 'Enhancing Cooperation Against Transborder Crime in SEE: What Are the Priorities?', Sofia, 28 February–2 March 2003.

NOTES

1. I cannot deal here with the urban legend about foreign (UN, NATO or EU) troops stationed within southeast Europe generating their own demand. There is no question that the supply of female prostitutes into the Balkans has been generated in part by the perception that the troops provide a market, but we have no counterfactual basis for assessing their independent effect. The issue in this case, moreover, is not with their causal role but with the appropriateness of instruments chosen for counteracting, managing and fighting the problem. As for UN, NATO or EU troops deployed into such situations, it is clear that they, too, need training in how to deal with local criminals or transborder organized crime and that peacekeepers do not yet receive such training.

2. Particularly explicit on these links is the study of Russia by Vadim Volkov (2002). He notes the turning point in 1998, when the chaos that entrepreneurs (the emerging capitalist class) found beneficial initially began to become increasingly costly and they began to want more predictable relations with the state. This shift in interests, combined with Putin's emphasis on state building, may be analogous to the role of business-led 'reform' governments in US cities in the early part of the twentieth century. See also Nikolov (1997).

3. Americans in this project, when interviewed, insisted that the money was laundered but that it was earned through sanctions busting, thus considered legitimate by them as part of an anti-Milošević activity, and not through trafficking in arms, drugs and humans.

4. In an Institute for War and Peace Reporting (IWPR) story about the attractiveness of prostitution to young women in Serbia, the average monthly wage in Serbia of 170 euro is contrasted to the 50 euro an hour, on average, that women in 'escort agencies' earn (Stijak 2003). To tackle smuggling of children in Albania, according to another IWPR report, 'researchers have concluded' that the best way 'is to take the children off the streets and find places for them in work programmes'. But NGOs actually doing this task find that one of the 'greatest problem[s]' they confront is the views of others toward the children – 'everybody despises' them (Loloçi 2002).

5. The obstacles to regional cooperation in southeast Europe are greater than the interests in its favour, according to the extensive empirical research by Othon Anastasakis and Vesna Bojičić-Dželilović. (2002).
6. They would have much support from Helga Konrad, chair of the Task Force on Trafficking in Human Beings of the Stability Pact. See her press statement (Konrad 2003) criticizing Montenegrin authorities over the lack of progress in the case of a Moldovan national, a trafficking victim, who surrendered herself to police authorities in November 2002.
7. See also the recent work by Margaret Levi on trust and the state.

REFERENCES

Anastasakis, Othon and Vesna Bojičić-Dželilović. (2002): *Balkan Regional Cooperation and European Integration* (London: The Hellenic Observatory, London School of Economics and Political Science).
Bardhan, Pranab (1997): 'Corruption and Development: A Review of Issues', *Journal of Economic Literature, 35* (September), pp.1320–46.
Haas, Peter M. (1992): 'Introduction: Epistemic Communities and International Policy Coordination', *International Organization, 46*:1, pp.1–36.
Hay, Douglas (1975): 'Property, Authority and the Criminal Law', in Douglas Hay et al., *Albion's Fatal Tree: Crime and Society in Eighteenth-Century England* (New York: Pantheon), pp.17–63.
Konrad, Helga (2003): 'Bring the Case to Court and Honour International Commitments', press statement, 10 February.
Loloçi, Çerçiz (2002): 'Albania: Police Arrest Child Traffickers', *Balkan Crisis Report 375*, 21 October.
Naim, Moisés (2003): 'The Five Wars of Globalization', *Foreign Policy, 134*, pp.29–36.
Nikolov, Jovo (1997): 'Crime and Corruption after Communism: Organized Crime in Bulgaria', *East European Constitutional Review, 6*:4, ⟨http://www.law.nyu.edu/eecr/vol6num4/feature/organizedcrime.html⟩.
Stijak, Slavisa (2003): 'Serbia: Booming Sex Trade Overwhelms Police', *Balkan Crisis Report 400*, 25 January.
United Nations Development Programme (1994): *Human Development Report 1994: New Dimensions of Human Security* (New York: Oxford University Press, 1994), available at ⟨http://www.undp.org/hdr⟩.
Volkov, Vadim (2002): *Violent Entrepreneurs: The Use of Force in the Making of Russian Capitalism* (Ithaca, NYand London: Cornell University Press).

Economic Perspectives on Organized Crime

KRASSEN STANCHEV

INTRODUCTION

A quick search through Google for 'drugs', 'organized crime' and 'Balkans' reveals that the 'black economy' is firmly associated with the region. The explanatory assumption appears to be: gangs of criminals drive southeast Europe into crime; it is intrinsic, and linked to international trade routes for drugs and other criminal activities. This underlying assumption is shared even by official documents. It is normal, there is crime and lawbreakers must be punished. Only rare voices call for a systemic and sober non-legalistic approach.

Among them, Lord Ashdown recognizes the reasons: the Balkan region is 'on Europe's frontier, it is the corridor for crime and criminal products from Asia and the Caucasus', it has weakened, fractured states and legal systems', and 'the black market – crime stalks after war' (Tomius 2002).

Another reasonable voice belongs to Mark Edmund Clark. He claims that:

> The operations of Balkans organized crime groups are nearly the same operations that one would see anywhere in the world. They provide goods and services in societies that the governments of those societies are unable to provide, may limit, or may restrict ... Balkan organized crime groups generally have functioned in complex networks that include: state security, intelligence, the military, political leaders, paramilitary groups, religious leaders, and business leaders in state-owned firms. They work in close cooperation to achieve mutual goals of increasing wealth and establishing greater influence in their states and sometimes other states within their region. (Clark 2003)

This brief overview is an attempt to cast some light on economic and systemic (i.e. political and economic) prerequisites of the organized crime in the Balkans, thus providing a different perspective. It speculates on issues such as the causes and provisional size of the black economy and semi-economic factors and constellations that have supported it in the last ten years.

LACK OF PROSPERITY

The post-Communist constellation in the Balkans dealt with the establishment of nation-states with clashes and controversies. Romania and Bulgaria share this background to some extent. They did not break with the past via 1990 elections and embarked on constitution making as form of legitimating new political establishments of both ex-communist and non-communist descent.

The dynamic of reform since then has been a stop-and-go process, only recently gaining simultaneous momentum in different countries. In the 1990s all the Balkan countries failed to provide for sustained economic growth and prosperity for a relatively long period; for Bulgaria not until 1998, for Romania not until 2000 (Table 1).

Whenever there was a period of growth, as in the Federal Republic of Yugoslavia between 1994 and 1998, or Bosnia and Herzegovina after 1994, it was insufficient to compensate for previous periods of decline and deconstruction. Even Bulgaria, which since 1997 has experienced its longest positive business cycle for the last 90 years, will only restore its pre-reform levels of per capita GDP in 2005.

The high growth levels in Albania and Bosnia and Herzegovina may be explained by accidental factors: Albanian development started from zero; figures for Bosnia and Herzegovina reflect international aid and post-war

TABLE 1
GDP GROWTH IN BALKAN COUNTRIES, 1991–2002

GDP growth (%)	1991	1992	1993	1994	1995	1996	1997	1998	1999	2000	2001	2002
Albania	−28	−7.2	9.6	8.3	13.3	9.1	−7	8	8	6.5	7.6	4.7
Bosnia–Herzegovina	–	–	–	32	50	69	30	18	8	5.5	4.4	5.5
Bulgaria	−11.7	−7.3	−1.5	1.8	2.9	−10.1	−7	3.5	2.4	5.8	4.1	4.8
Croatia	−21.1	−11.1	−8	5.9	6.8	5.9	6.8	2.5	−0.3	2.5	3.8	5.2
Macedonia	−3.2	−8.2	−1.2	−1.8	−1.1	1.2	1.4	2.9	2.7	5	−4.5	0.3
Romania	−12.9	−8.8	1.5	3.9	7.1	3.9	−6.1	−5.4	−3.2	1	5.7	4.9
Yugoslavia (SCG)	−11.6	−27.9	−30.8	2.5	6.1	5.9	7.4	2.5	−23.2	7	5.1	3.0

Source: National statistics, IMF (for Albania and Bosnia and Herzegovina), own calculations.

reconstruction. The Yugoslav successor states experienced disruption in their development, mostly attributable to crisis and civic conflict. (There are exceptions. The government of Macedonia followed consistent economic policies and was not responsible for the crisis of 2001; on the other hand, being relatively small in size, the government of Albania failed to provide for national security in 1997 and its lack of attention to institutional reforms and rule of law was one of the background reasons for the crisis of 1997.)

International comparisons suggest that organized economic crime has every chance to remain endemic in the region for a long time). Table 2

TABLE 2
SIZE OF ECONOMY AND OTHER INDICATORS FOR BALKAN STATES

Country	2002 real GDP (euro)	2002 GDP as % of 1989	Private sector % of GDP	FDI ($US millions)		Registered unemployment (June 2003)
				Cumulative	Per capita	
Albania	5,474	121	75	936	303	15.2
Bosnia–Herzegovina	5,450	54	45	753	198	43
Bulgaria	16.527	80	75	4,390	560	13.7
Croatia	23,620	87	60	6,296	1,419	18.9
Macedonia	39,18	76	60	935	467	46
Romania	48,384	87	65	9,008	415	7.1
Yugoslavia (SCG)	16,601	50	45	1,717	206	29
Total/average	119,874	79.2	60.7	3,433	509	24.7

Note: Data for Bosnia and Herzegovina is only for the Federation; the figure for Serbia and Montenegro is for the first half of 2002 and excludes Kosovo and Metohia.

Source: National statistics, EBRD, UNECE.

summarizes economic indicators that help provide an economic explanation for the background of organized crime.

The size of the combined real GDP of the region is rather small. For comparison, the GDP of the Czech Republic in 2002 was 43.3 per cent of the total GDP of all seven Balkan countries. It is obvious that none of the countries, other than Albania, managed to reach their 1989 GDP level. This is in contrast to the ex-Communist countries that recently joined the EU; their average 2002 GDP was 101.4 per cent of the 1989 value. Memories of previous prosperity, whatever its source was, must be vivid, causing discontent. The proximity of Europe allows for unfavorable comparison: for Bulgaria and Romania the per capita GDP in 2002 was about 25 per cent of the EU average and for the rest of the Balkans (excluding Croatia) it was about one-fifth of that level. It is also obvious that the restoration of previous GDP levels is much slower in the Yugoslavia successor states, again excluding Croatia, than in the EU accession countries.

On average, Balkan countries, excluding Bulgaria and Romania, maintain sizable government sectors with chronic inefficiency and artificial employment and causing sizable fiscal deficits – ranging in 2002 from 4.5 per cent in Bosnia and Herzegovina to 6.3 per cent in Albania (EBRD 2003: 59).

The total level of foreign direct investment (FDI) in southeast Europe is $24,035 million; it is almost the same as Hungary's cumulative FDI or 65.6 per cent of the FDI of the Czech Republic. These figures demonstrate that with few exceptions the countries do not provide proper investment and prosperity options, that proximity to the EU is not a sufficient factor for interweaving the economies and that there is as yet no critical mass of foreign interest to help change the overall economic patterns and frameworks. The EBRD does not count Croatia as part of southeast Europe. According to the most recent EBRD assessment, the region attracts nine per cent of cumulative FDI to former planned economies and 74 per cent of this is concentrated in Bulgaria and Romania (EBRD 2003: 90).

Average unemployment in central and eastern Europe (excluding the CIS) is 14.8 per cent, compared to 8.7 per cent in the EU. According to UNECE, in the last year and a half there has been a decline in unemployment only in Albania, Bulgaria and Croatia (UNECE 2003: 23). It is to be expected that the region will sustain its disadvantageous position and will retain incentives for migration and illegal economic activity.

Starting a legitimate business is also far from easy. Table 3 shows a comparison between Balkan business registration patterns and t e best EU practice for establishing a limited liability company. The countries with the most expensive registration systems, Albania and Bosnia and

TABLE 3
COMPANY REGISTRATION IN THE BALKANS AND BEST PRACTICE BENCHMARK,
2003

	Steps to register an LLC	Days	Formal costs (€)	Minimum paid-up capital (€)
Albania	11	62	655	770
Bosnia–Herzegovina	12	74	656	2,560 (local)
				5,100 (foreign)
Bulgaria	10	30	132	2,560
Croatia	13	50	746	2,560
Macedonia	7	48	240	2,500 (local)
				5,000 (foreign)
Montenegro (SCG)	4	4	11	1
Romania	v9	46	579	60
Serbia (SCG)	16	71	194	5,000
Best practice	1	3	210	3,000

Source: World Bank, EU Commission/

Herzegovina, where according to the World Bank the costs of registering are equal to 62 and 55 per cent, respectively, of per capita gross national income, are the most reluctant to changes their procedures.

SPECULATIVE ILLUSTRATIONS OF THE SHADOW ECONOMY

There is no shortage of government institutions, international initiatives and programmes to address organized crime in the Balkans. At the same, there are few publicly available and quantitative estimates of the size of the 'black economy' of the region. The closest similar phenomenon is the shadow economy. An upcoming publication summarizes the available research for the Balkans (Dimitrov et al. n.d.). It gives some useful insights on the matter. Table 4 should be taken only as a sample summarizing some of the key surveys. It is not representative by any means and might taken only as insight for speculative calculations, taken with a pinch of salt.

The general impression is that in Bulgaria, Romania and Macedonia the 'shadow' economy with its ups and downs contributed to a prominent and expanding growing percentage of GDP during the period 1990–2000. In the case of Croatia the 'gray' economy appears to stay close to its initial level from the beginning of transition. The available estimates for Albania, Bosnia (Republika Srpska) and Serbia and Montenegro more or less indicate the levels of the 'shadow' economy in individual years but are

TABLE 0ESTIMATES OF THE SIZE OF THE INFORMAL ECONOMY AS PERCENTAGE
OF GDP

	1990		1995		1999/2000	
	1990–1993	1990				
Albania	–	–	–	81[i]	33.4[a]	–
Bosnia–Herzegovina	n.a.	–	56.3[d]	–	34.1[a]	51.2[d]
Bulgaria	27.1[b]	29.6[h]	34[c]	81.5[h]	36.9[a]	40.8[h]
Croatia	24.6[b]	.	36[c]	25[e]	33.4[a]	25.3[e]
Macedonia	35.6[b]	–	44.2[c]	–	45.1[b]	–
Romania	27.3[b]	21.3[f]	28.3[c]	28.5[f]	34.4[a]	37.2[f]
Serbia and Montenegro	–	31.6[g]	–	40.8[g]	29.1[a]	34.5[g]

[a]Schneider (2002b: 13); informal economy in percentage of GNP. The author is relying on the currency demand, physical input and DYMIMIC (dynamic multiple-indicators multiple causes) approaches.

[b]Schneider (2002a: 7. The author applied the DYMIMIC approach.

[c]Lacko (2000), applying the physical input method.

[d]Tomas (2000: 36). Data are only for Republika Srpska; applying the labour market approach. Bosnia–Herzegovina figures are 1996.

[e]Šošić and Faulend (2002: 69). Applying the monetary method.

[f]Dobrescu (2000). Applying the physical input approach.

[g]Krstic (1998). Applying the labour market approach. Serbia and Montenegro figures are 1991 and 1997.

[h]Kyle et al. (2001). applying the physical input approach, labour market approach and monetary method. Croatia figures are 1998.

[i]Eilat and Zinnes (2000). Applying the model approach.

not extended enough for measuring dynamics. The years after 2000 can be perceived as rather normal, without the impact of wars and embargoes.

The shadow economy, broadly defined as unregistered activity, embraces 'black' economic activities, i.e. those criminalized by law and not registered due to this fact. If we take, rather conservatively, two provisional sizes of the informal economy of the Balkans in recent years, we can use two estimated – of 30 and 40 per cent of the total Balkan GDP. Assuming that the per capita GDP is around €120, the shadow economy would be €36 billion in the first estimate and €48 billion according to the second. For the sake of benchmarking, we can assume that the 'black' economy is 10 per cent of the 'gray', shadow or informal economy.

What is important in this thought experiment is not the verification – measurements and field research would be eventually undertaken or made public if available. What matters is the size of the incentives expected and/or created by the black economy. The respective speculative guesses of the share of the criminal economic activities (say, of €3.6 and €4.8 billion) might be compared with available figures of GDP per capita, FDI or foreign aid and/or be viewed as potential income of the unemployed. Even if the assumption is that the 'black' segment of the shadow economy is five per cent, any speculation would speak of strikingly important motivation for criminal entrepreneurship.

SOME FINAL REMARKS

To understand the causes of the rise of organized crime in southeast Europe we need to look at the political and security developments in the area in the late 1980s and in the 1990s. Organized crime in southeast Europe has little to do with the old, familiar historical forces of the Balkans. Therefore there is no point in demonizing them.

Nation building in the former republics of Yugoslavia provided a paramount cause for conflict and interfered with normal economic processes and intra-regional exchange. The embargoes necessitated by the wars and the eventual dismissal of the armies exacerbated the problem. Conditions of civic war, and violent nation-building led to criminalization of trade and economic activities. The wars in former Yugoslavia had predictable impacts on economic exchange. The demand for banned products and services exploded along with increased demand for resources to finance these products and services. The wars eradicated the rule of law and 'invited' black market vendors and embargo violators from neighbouring and more distant countries.

Those who benefited from these new 'opportunities' were the old or revamped ex-Yugoslav power elites, the army and paramilitary groups. The disappearance of the paternalistic state and the dissolution of Yugoslavia had released idle 'cadres' with special skills in violence, sharing a high degree of inter-group trust and faced with little competition either from the home government or from the international community. Needless to say, their networks spread across the region, corrupting customs and other government bodies. If one looks at post-Dayton problems of customs and business reforms in Bosnia and Herzegovina, it would become clear how difficult it was (and is) to overcome that legacy of the wars.

The undecided status of Kosovo and the failure to organize representative democracy is reproducing the model of *chetnik* (i.e. guerilla) tactics of late nineteenth- and early twentieth-century national movements. These tactics revitalize political rhetoric and interethnic conflicts of the past, jeopardize the fragile trust upon which business is built and scare businessmen and foreign investment away from the region. As Arben

Xhaferi put it more bluntly: 'I explain [the outbreak of violence in Macedonia] as ethnic competition: to whom does the state belong?' (IWPR 1971).

Organized crime control-seeking policies have to be international but in the case of southeast Europe such policies were applied by the international community on a country-by-country basis with dubious results. In the case of Kosovo, UNMIK seems to malfunction. If there are positive developments, they result not from intentional policies to contain crime but rather from processes of converging black economic activities into shadow and 'white' entrepreneurship.

It has become obvious that coordinated international action against Balkan organized crime is virtually impossible. It requires a multi-dimensional approach: first, in western Europe (except perhaps Spain, Scandinavia and the UK) the authorities should address both the demand for black services and products originated in the Balkans; second, the carrot and stick approach including EU accession for the countries of the western Balkans should be employed; and third, there should be concerted international cooperation to support local national efforts to eliminate formal and informal structures linked to organized crime.

There are very few reasons to give rise to optimism regarding winning the battle against organized crime in the Balkans. One of them, however, is that it is currently spreading into neighbouring countries relatively slowly in comparison with the time of the UN embargo on Yugoslavia and the Greece embargo on Macedonia (the period before 1995). Another reason is that the political/security conditions which allowed crime to rise in the early 1990s are still to be found only in Kosovo and Bosnia and Herzegovina. Therefore, organised crime in southeast Europe can be contained, at least to some extent.

REFERENCES

Clark, Mark E. (2003): 'Understanding Balkan Organized Crime: A Key to Success in Iraq?', interview on Columbia International Affairs Online, July, ⟨http://www.ciaonet.org/special_section/iraq/papers/clm10/clm10.html⟩.

Dimitrov, Martin, Assenka Yonkova-Hristova, Georgi Stoeff and Yordanka Gancheva (n.d.): *Overview of Research on the Size of the Informal Economy in SEE* (Athens: ELIAMEP).

Dobrescu, Emilian (2000): *Macro Models of the Romanian Transition Economy*, 2nd and 3rd eds.

EBRD (2003): *Transition Report 2003: Integration and Regional Cooperatioon*. London: European Bank for Reconstruction and Development.

Eilat, Yair and Clifford Zinnes (2000): *The Evolution of the Shadow Economy in Transition Countries: Consequences for Economic Growth and Donor Assistance*, CAER II Discussion Paper No.83. Cambridge, MA: Harvard Institute for International Development. Available at ⟨http://www.cid.harvard.edu/caer2/htm/content/papers/paper83/paper83.pdf⟩.

IWPR (2001): 'An Optimist in Panic: An Interview with Arben Xhaferi', ⟨http://www.greekhelsinki.gr/bhr/english/countries/macedonia/iwpr_07_04_01.html⟩.

Krstic, G. (1998): *Analysis of the Hidden Economy in FR Yugoslavia with Estimates for 1997 and Recommendations for its Legalization*. Belgrade: Economics Institute.

Kyle, S., A. Warner, L. Dimitrov, R. Krustev, S. Alexandrova and K. Stanchev (2001): *The 'Shadow' Economy in Bulgaria*. Ithaca, NY and Boston, MA: Cornell University Agency for Economic Analysis and Forcasting and Harvard University Institute for Market Economics.

Lacko, Mari (2000): 'Hidden Economy – An Unknown Quantity? Comparative Analysis of Hidden Economies in Transition Countries in 1989–1995', *Economics of Transition*, 8:1, pp.117–49.

Schneider, Friedrich (2002a): *The Size and Development of the Shadow Economies and Shadow Economy Labour Force of 22 Transition and 21 OECD Countries: What do we really know?*, Discussion Paper No.514. Bonn: Institute for the Study of Labour. http://papers.ssrn.com/sol3/papers.cfm?abstract_id=320083

Schneider, Friedrich (2002b): *Size and Measurement of the Informal Economy in 110 Countries around the World*, Washington, DC: World Bank Rapid Response Unit.

Šošić, Vedran and Michael Faulend (2002): *Dollarization and the Underground Economy: Accidental Partners?* Zagreb: Institute of Public Finance.

Tomas, Rajko (2000): *Volume, Structure and Methods to Eliminate the Grey Economy in Republika Srpska*.

Tomius, Eugen (2002): 'Balkans: Officials Pledge to Tackle the "Cancer" of Organized Crime', Radio Free Europe/Radio Liberty, 26 November, ⟨http://www.rferl.org/features/2002/11/26112002165722.asp⟩.

UNECE (2003): *Economic Survey of Europe, 2003*, No 2. Geneva: United Nations Economic Commission for Europe.

Migration Policies of Western European Governments and the Fight Against Organized Crime in SEE

MISHA GLENNY

Southeast Europe (SEE) is the key front-line transit region for the delivery into the European Union of illegal products of whatever ilk and origin. Not only is it the springboard for the trafficking of women who either come from the region or its near neighbours, it is also an important route for products arriving from other parts of the world, be it heroin transfer from Afghanistan and Burma, cigarettes that originate in many different places (including ironically the EU whither they are bound to return), or guns from eastern Europe, Russia and even as far afield as South America. It is an important regional money-laundering centre, and above all, it is the point from where a huge number of illegal immigrants actually cross into the European Union. This diversity of services makes SEE especially profitable for organized crime, and it is well established that one form of criminal activity will piggyback on another – different products are generally delivered along the same routes.

The anthropological and historical reasons for this are relatively well understood in theory, although actual field research is fragmented and anecdotal, not least because this can be a hazardous undertaking. Nonetheless, it is generally assumed that the extended family structure which is especially prevalent in the southern Balkans assists the development of flexible and loyal networks that are extremely difficult to penetrate and are easily disguised. With regard to historical tradition, the Balkans was always ideal for the flowering of crime and smuggling as imperial borderlands characterized by sustained underdevelopment.

Just as modern weaponry has helped transform low-level vendetta politics into mass murder in SEE, so have modern forms of transport and communication proved an immensely useful tool for multiplying the profits of smugglers and criminals. Another advantage enjoyed by the criminal elites is their very size – they are small, and, in the western Balkans, they have been able paradoxically to ignore largely the economic and political disadvantages caused by the fragmentation of the former Yugoslavia – they retain and nurture old contacts and have few cultural problems in sustaining good professional cooperation. As small groups, they are much less constrained by national or communal tensions than the legitimate political elites are (even given a certain degree of crossover between the criminal and the legitimate). Indeed, nationalism is a convenient tool which they are prepared to mobilize if they feel that their business interests are threatened (the clearest example of this was in Macedonia), but for the most part they represent a paragon of the intercommunal and interethnic cooperation for whose absence the Balkans is otherwise so renowned.

These are, however, chiefly operational matters that explain the impressive success rate of organized criminal gangs or the mafia in the Balkans. The underlying cause for their continued growth lies in high rates of unemployment, stagnant legitimate economies and in the failure of either domestic or international political actors to have any significant impact on the economic situation in SEE. Add this to the geo-economic reality that sees SEE nestled cheek-by-jowl next to what is soon to be the largest and most affluent market in history (one, moreover, that has developed a seemingly insatiable appetite for prostitutes, drugs, untaxed cigarettes, small arms and cheap labour), and you have conditions as near as perfect as one might imagine for the blossoming of a crime-driven society.

In the long term, the answer to the problem of organized crime can only be found in systematically addressing this problem. But there is a short-term issue whose satisfactory resolution can alleviate matters to a degree that will have a material impact on the development prospects of SEE. This is the sensitive subject of immigration into the EU, or more specifically access to the labour markets of the EU for citizens of SEE and the western Balkans in particular.

Meeting in Tampere in October 1999, the European Council agreed that member states would work towards the convergence of immigration and asylum policies, in part to introduce clarity for their own citizens regarding these highly sensitive issues, and in part to secure the long-term labour needed for economic growth and stability in the EU. There is widespread agreement among member states and between ministries that a coherent and detailed policy of migration management is absolutely crucial to the EU's ability to maintain and strengthen its global economic position. While rhetoric often coincides, political practice rarely does, particularly on an issue that has such a powerful and unpredictable impact on electoral politics, as does immigration. Indeed, there are few areas of policy where EU policy makers' strategic goals and requirements are so far adrift from public perceptions and discourse – this is where the democratic deficit of the EU is perhaps at its most damaging.

The need of member state governments to placate popular and media hostility to immigration and asylum means that the coordination of migration policy remains at a low level and public disputes – as, for example, between Britain and France over the Sangatte refugee centre – are much more visible than any major steps towards a common policy. This also means that initiatives that hint at the liberalization of most aspects of migration policy very quickly run into difficulties with their core directorate and ministries – justice and home affairs. While there has been important progress under the presidency of Romano Prodi in broadening the issue to include other directorates and ministries in considering migration policy, it is the concerns of domestic interior ministries which bring the greatest influence to bear on policy. In recent years, we have witnessed throughout the European Union how politicians have been vying with one another to assume the most uncompromising line on asylum and immigration. This phenomenon has now surfaced in countries, such as Ireland or Sweden, that have been free in the past from such stormy and sometimes distressing debates.

Within the European Council and the Commission, there is a clear recognition of the urgent need for a well-managed migration policy in order to rejuvenate its labour force that is ageing due to declining birth rates and improving geriatric health care. This is not an issue where the EU can afford to reflect on for very long because it is already imposing a strain on the pensions system. Even in the United Kingdom, which has gone relatively far down the road of pensions reform, the pattern of ageing has had a severe effect on the pension industry's ability to meet its commitments. Germany, in particular, is likely to face a crisis of massive proportions in a decade or so if it does not address the need for pension reform.

Despite this need, Europe's tradition of absorbing relatively few immigrants (in striking contrast to the United States, which actively seeks out immigrants to replenish its labour stock) has led to a strong cultural resistance to the idea of even modest policies of managed immigration. Levels of legal immigration remain relatively low. In Britain, France and Germany, figures over the five years to 2002 hover between 100,000 and 225,000 net immigrants in each country. But these include several significant anomalies – return of the *Volksdeutsche*, for example, who are often of a non-productive age, or in the case of the UK a large number of family dependents joining immigrants already there.

Despite its proximity to the EU, despite the cultural links between it and EU member states, and despite the cheap but relatively well-educated labour force that it offers, immigration from SEE into the EU remains exceptionally low as a percentage. This is often a result of culturally specific factors obtaining in individual member states. In the United Kingdom in 2001, for example, only 12.2 per cent (15,100) of all legally-registered immigrants (123,000) were from non-EEA states in Europe. Of this 12.2 per cent, roughly 10 per cent came from SEE. The UK actively searches for immigrants, largely in the IT, healthcare and teaching sectors, from former colonies, now members of the Commonwealth, arguing (on those rare occasions when it is called to do so) that familiarity with English makes these areas natural partners. France, too, prefers to seek its immigrants from francophone countries and others where it retains colonial or cultural links. Only Germany registers a relatively higher absorption of immigrants from SEE (especially from Serbia and Montengro), although it is still low in percentage terms. So far, however, the proclaimed EU policy of managed migration has not extended into strategic cooperation in terms of the origin of immigrants. The relationship between unemployment and organised crime in SEE has not yet crossed into the discourse over visas and the labour market. Yet from a practical point of view, the economic stabilisation of SEE brings the EU more benefits more quickly than would similar processes elsewhere.

This low level of immigration from SEE has not prevented the emergence of some extremely negative stereotypes in many parts of the EU. Although hard to quantify, this phenomenon has, I believe, contributed significantly to the persistence of a strong sense of antipathy felt towards the Balkans and its peoples in several member states. The success of Albanian organized crime groups in major cities throughout southern and northern Europe has led to the rapid characterization of the Albanian mafia as being the most ruthless and successful in Europe. Even in the

United Kingdom, where Yardies from Jamaica control the cocaine trade and Turkish and Kurdish clans clash for dominance in the importation of heroin, Albanians from both Albania and Kosovo have become the standard symbol of the new wave of organized crime, followed in popular perceptions by Romanian criminals and a supposed army of petty Roma thieves.

In general, the EU has confirmed or in some cases made harder access to the EU for Balkan citizens, partly out of fear that the criminal gangs can exploit exemptions on visa regimes. The argument is partially flawed inasmuch as borders pose little or no problem for organized criminals from the Balkans – indeed one might describe the illegal transportation of goods and people across borders to be their core business. There is, however, no doubt that the ease with which one can obtain passports in some SEE countries could be construed as a legitimate security threat within the EU.

Nonetheless, the arguments for easing access of SEE citizens to EU labour markets are compelling and clearly mutually beneficial. The economic requirements of the SEE and the EU are complementary – the latter needs to replenish its labour force, the former needs to alleviate unemployment and find ways of injecting liquidity into local economies. In a system of managed migration, workers are removed from criminal activities, they pay taxes in the host country, they contribute to their own economy both in terms of remittances and in returning home with skills learned in a more dynamic labour market.

But with specific regard to the Balkans, there is an additional imperative which I consider of immense significance. The integration of SEE into European structures represents a massive challenge but also an opportunity for both the region and the EU. At a time of political division and great uncertainty, the need for the stabilization of SEE is relatively uncontroversial – the benefits are obvious just as failure to succeed threatens hair-raising consequences, both in the area of social and communal unrest and in the domain of organized crime.

As opinion both in the western Balkans and, more slowly, in Brussels and member state capitals comes round to the idea that the Stabilisation and Association process needs to offer greater incentives to the region if it is to help galvanize local social and economic development, the issue of increased labour market access should be integrated into any revision of the relationship between the EU and SEE.

One is hardly likely to underestimate the difficulty in persuading Brussels or member states that increased market access for SEE citizens would be a good thing. I do not mean to single out Germany for bad practice, it is merely that its faults are particularly illuminating when it comes to the issue of economic migration. Its insistence that Polish citizens would be denied access to the German labour market for seven years after Poland joins the EU in 2004 sends out a very negative signal. Even more disturbing is how, when Germany tried to woo IT specialists from India and eastern Europe with long-term visas (after a campaign in which one opposition leader tried to block the move using explicitly racist arguments), the take up was about one in four of the visas on offer. Europe is now perceived by highly skilled migrant labour as being both unwelcoming and hostile to enterprise.

Currently only citizens of Bulgaria and Romania enjoy limited access through the provision conferred on citizens of accession countries allowing them to establish themselves in the EU as self-employed workers. In theory, this means that there should be no hindrance to a Bulgarian plumber or a Romanian translator from setting up a business in Munich or Toulouse. Of course, Romania, Bulgaria and Croatia also enjoy a visa-free regime with the Schengen area.

In the immediate future, the remaining countries in the western Balkans are unlikely to be granted similar visa-free privileges. I would argue that it would be tactless for the western Balkan countries to make this demand, and almost certainly doomed to end in failure.

But there are two areas where the EU and the region could swiftly develop fruitful cooperation. The first is with the establishment of a regime of short-term contracts for work in the service, manufacturing and agriculture sectors. If SEE citizens were allowed to take employment for a limited period (without necessarily enjoying the right of moving their family), they would contribute to overcoming the perennial problem of finding a seasonal workforce (and now that the next ten are about to become EU members, this will leave a large dent in this part of the labour market). This is a scheme which already finds great favour among employers in the EU. But it will also help to reduce one of the problems that migration creates inside SEE, that is the loss of skills or brain drain. In fact, a policy of carefully enforced temporary labour permits for SEE citizens would see an increase in dynamic economic activity that is already visible in traditionally high areas of emigration such as Greece or among the Albanian populations.

Another simple but easily manageable policy shift would be to confer the rights to establish self-employed businesses for citizens of the western Balkans. I can only here speak anecdotally about the experience of the United Kingdom, but my country is now suffering a serious shortage of workers in mobile service trades such as plumbing, painting and decorating. The only employment sector where the citizens of some western Balkan countries have ready access to is au pairing. According to UK statistics, the number of au pairs from Croatia, Macedonia and Bulgaria is increasing the fastest, apparently because they are more prepared to knuckle down than the increasingly pampered au pairs from the Czech Republic, Poland and Slovakia.

Women's access to the EU labour markets has perhaps the most obvious impact on the reduction of organized crime. The gender studies department at Warsaw University has offered convincing evidence that a great majority of Polish and other East European women who go to Germany and elsewhere to work as prostitutes are fully aware of what they are getting themselves into. Their goal is either to escape the poverty trap or to provide for families in areas of high unemployment. While undoubtedly an appalling indictment of European society, the more dramatic stories of abduction, rape and enforced prostitution are less common than may at first be apparent.

None of this seeks to deny the role of policing with regard to the struggle against organised crime in SEE. It is merely to highlight that policing alone will not solve this problem. As part of its presidency focus on SEE, the Greek Foreign Ministry has, together with the US-based Migration Policy Institute, established a working group, the Athens Migration Policy Initiative, which is currently in the process of formulating concrete proposals both for Brussels and member states to consider. If these prove sufficiently cogent and if the complex process of mobilising constituencies within the EU to create a robust political coalition were to succeed, such an initiative could have a critical impact in curtailing the Balkan mafias' access to its key resource – labour.

ACKNOWLEDGEMENTS

An earlier version of this article was presented at ELIAMEP's workshop on 'Enhancing Cooperation Against Transborder Crime in SEE: What are the Priorities?', 28 February–2 March 2003, Sofia.

Fighting Organized Crime in a UN Protectorate: Difficult, Possible, Necessary

RADOSLAVA STEFANOVA

OVERVIEW

Four years since the end of NATO's air campaign against the former Yugoslavia, conducted to stop the cleansing of ethnic Albanians by the Milošević regime, Kosovo is increasingly cited in relation to organized crime (Prentice 1999; Seper 1999: 1; Fleishman 1999; Politi 1999; Milivojevic 1995). According to *The Washington Post*, 'during the past three years, Kosovo has become the European capital for trafficking in human beings, and the most important transit point for drug smuggling on the continent' (Bardos 2002). *The Economist* recently recounted the former Yugoslav province in terms of its 'notorious underworld, in which dealers in prostitutes, heroin, cigarettes and guns have made vast fortunes', and pointed out that organized crime there proves to be more difficult to contain than elsewhere (*Economist* 2002). *The Wall Street Journal* speculated about terrorist connections in Kosovo, and reported the possibility of some Al Qaeda involvement through suspect Muslim charities (Phelps 2002).[1] The UN-run International Police in Kosovo reported that 'organized crime and official corruption remain problems that threaten the stability of Kosovo, and the tools needed to address the problems are not yet in place' (*UNMIK Police Annual Report*, 5 December 2002). In fact, it would not be exaggerated to claim that the predominantly Albanian-populated province of the former Yugoslav federation (currently named 'Serbia and Montenegro') harbours some of the most influential criminal elements in the Balkans, and oversees much of the illegal trafficking flows in and out of the region. Organized crime in the Balkans is a problem so serious that according to a report of the Council for Foreign Relations, it needs to be considered on equal grounds to that of global terrorism. The same report urges the safeguarding of US vital interests by contributing more actively to combating what appears to be an unrestrained criminality in the region (Dao 2002).

This state of affairs in Kosovo is, to an extent, paradoxical, since the province has been a de facto UN protectorate since June 1999, when NATO troops entered there following the defeat of former Yugoslav President Milošević by the allied bombing campaign. Currently the UN administers the province with the help of about 25,000 NATO soldiers and roughly 4,000 UN civilian police (CIVPOL) officers (*UNMIK Police Daily Press Update*, 17 July 2003). This compact presence of international military and police expertise stands out in contrast to the neighbouring countries' own rather weak institutions employed in the fight against organized crime.

With the prospect of an eventual solution to Kosovo's undefined status in mind, it is necessary to consider the repercussions of the creation of yet another Balkan entity where organized criminal groups might have significant influence on institutions, as well as more broadly on regional politics. This has long been a worry of senior US diplomats concerned with a definitive decision regarding Kosovo's status (author's interviews with US Foreign Service officers in Rome, February 2001). The key fear is that institutions dominated by organized crime might easily yield to pressure from actors whose economic interests could drive the region back into violent conflict, and make it a convenient base for terrorists worldwide. This fear is shared also by a number of high-profile figures in Kosovo society itself.[2] Four years since its establishment, the UN interim administration in Kosovo (UNMIK) finally recognized the seriousness of the problem. Hence it included in its general list of crucial benchmarks to be achieved by the nascent local institutions of self-governance (PISG) before Kosovo's status is to be discussed, a requirement pertaining to the fight against organized crime.[3]

This article examines UNMIK's institutional preparedness to fight organized crime, as well as the latter's roots and known manifestations. Particular attention is devoted to four major components of criminal profit-making activities: drugs and arms trade, human trafficking, and financial fraud. To the extent to which evidence was found, the topic of organized crime's influence on Kosovo's politics is also discussed. Finally, some policy suggestions are put forward with a view to redressing some institutional and legal shortcomings in the current international management of the fight against organized crime.

KOSOVO AND THE BALKAN CRIMINAL NETWORKS

Prior to the disintegration of Yugoslavia, the main transit route for the criminal transfer of goods and people passed through Turkey, Bulgaria, Serbia and Slovenia, and into Austria, Germany and the rest of Western Europe. The Yugoslav wars provided better opportunities for traffickers as they took advantage of the law enforcement vacuum in the FRY and began to pass goods primarily through Serbia, Kosovo, Albania or Montenegro, and via the Adriatic, to Italy and western Europe (Milivojevic 1995).

In the late 1990s, ethnic Albanian fighters of the Kosovo Liberation Army (KLA) turned to organized crime to fund their struggle against the Serbian authorities.[4] The guerrillas thus established several coordinating centres for regional criminal activity in and around Kosovo, notably for drugs, arms and human trafficking.[5] Many suspect that a substantial portion of Balkan criminal activity is dominated by the extended Kosovo Albanian families.[6] In fact, criminal networks based on kinship, such as the ones operating from Kosovo, are particularly difficult for the police to penetrate and neutralize due to the strong blood bonds and clan allegiance not normally found in criminal formations linked predominantly by mutual interest for profit (for a detailed discussion, see Bovenkerk 2001; Paoli 2001).

In view of the fact that at least some KLA funding was procured through organized crime, and due to the strong continuity between the former KLA and part of the current Kosovo political and executive establishment, speculation naturally arises of how influential criminal elements within and outside of the province are in today's Kosovo politics. While there is no hard evidence directly linking the main political parties to organized crime (mostly because the clan structure of the society in Kosovo makes it practically impossible for witnesses to testify without seriously endangering themselves and their families[7] or for local police to investigate into the matter (*UNMIK Police Annual Report*, 5 December

2002)), the nature and the amount of intercepted organized criminal activity in Kosovo indicate that such speculations are clearly within the realm of the possible.

Furthermore, the extent and the scope of intercepted criminal activities in Kosovo indicate that organized crime networks in the Balkans are also an interethnic enterprise. The Balkans' geopolitical location at the crossroads between Asia and Europe has made it a old-time haven for illegal trafficking. In addition, weak institutions and chronic underdevelopment in the neighbouring countries strengthened the trans-Balkans crime networks, which often find allies in some governments and public administrations in the region. As the consequences of organized crime in the Balkans are being felt across Europe and in the United States,[8] and as its detrimental impact on regional development becomes evident (Davis, Hirst and Mariani 2001), it is important to understand what is being done to counter crime in Kosovo, where, unlike elsewhere in the region, one finds a concentration of international aid[9] and expertise managed by the UN.

UNMIK'S EFFORTS

Organized criminal activity in Kosovo appears to be well rooted and has flourished for at least a decade (see also Politi 1999), nevertheless, the establishment of UNMIK, and notably of CIVPOL after the 1999 NATO military campaign, played an important role in limiting criminal activities in the province (*Economist* 2002). The presence of NATO's Kosovo Force (KFOR), as well as of the UN civilian police, is responsible for the partial relocation of trafficking in smuggled goods and people farther south to Macedonia and west to Albania and Montenegro. However, it is worth noting that criminal groups from Kosovo appear to dominate regional organized crime and to retain a substantial portion of the profits (Layne 1999; Chazan 1994).

Particularly since 2002, fighting organized crime has become a top UNMIK and KFOR priority, one increasingly seen as crucial for successful institution building, economic development and political stability.[10] However, the international administration has had limited success in finding and dismantling criminal rings. The few in dictments related to organized crime have been restricted to specific activities, such as prostitution and people trafficking, despite the fact that it is often apparent that the same individuals are also involved in a whole chain of other illegal activities, such as money laundering, arms smuggling and drug trafficking. The police have so far been unable to link these activities to a broader network.[11]

Besides the objective difficulties in operating in traditional societies such as the one in Kosovo, problems also have to do with the fact that specialized units dedicated to fighting organized crime have only recently been created; for example, the Kosovo Organized Crime Bureau (KOCB) was established in late 2001. As most institutions in Kosovo, these units are headed and run by internationals who find it more difficult to penetrate local crime circles than their colleagues operating in their native lands, due to lack of linguistic and other local knowledge, as well as due to the general difficulty of serving in a multinational UN environment rather than under a single government. In addition, the legal framework to fight organized crime is still incomplete. Investigations often remain entangled in turf battles between the police and the judiciary, with resultant bureaucratic inefficiency, which appears to be a particularly serious problem within the UN structures (author's interviews with senior UN police professionals, October and November 2002). In order to fully understand these problems, as well as the difficulties in addressing them, it is worth exploring the most diffused criminal activities in Kosovo.

MAJOR AREAS OF ORGANIZED CRIME ACTIVITY IN KOSOVO

Drugs

Kosovo has traditionally been a major transit point on the drug routes from Central Asia and the Middle East to western Europe. As mentioned, the violent disintegration of the old Yugoslavia boosted the drug trade in and from the province, since at least some KLA armament was financed by drug money (Politi 1999: 55; Times 1999; Seper 1999; Prentice 1999). Although domestic demand for drugs has increased over the last two years, the deployment of KFOR patrols along Kosovo's borders and the general presence of UNMIK police have somewhat deterred the free flow of narcotics, as drug barons have evidently switched bulkier shipments to routes through Greece, Macedonia, Albania and Montenegro (author's interviews with police drug investigators and senior police investigative staff, March, April, May, July and August, 2002; UNMIK Police Annual Report, 5 December 2002). A specific Drug Trafficking Unit (DTU) within the Central Criminal Investigation Unit (CCIU) of UNMIK Police was only established in June 2001, i.e. two years after the UN took charge of the administration of the province. In fact, senior investigative officers often point out that much of the police inefficiency in deterring the trafficking flows has to do with a particularly bureaucratic authorization and decision-making process within the UN (author's interviews with senior international police officers at UNMIK, March, April, May, July, August and November 2002).

The DTU consists of a core coordination unit exclusively staffed by internationals, and five regional coordinating units with mixed international police officers and local (overwhelmingly Albanian) Kosovo Police Service (KPS) officers. Local police involvement in the drug investigations has been necessary, because most of the international officers do not speak the local languages. However, KPS officers are also particularly vulnerable to both social pressure from Kosovo's traditional society not to investigate against their ethnic brethren, and to threats from organized crime (author's interviews with senior international police officers at UNMIK; *UNMIK Police Annual Report*, 5 December 2002). As a result, police success in intercepting drug trafficking in Kosovo has had mixed results.

The major drugs that are being seized in Kosovo are marijuana, hashish,[12] and heroin. Small quantities of cocaine, morphine and amphetamine have also been confiscated. Due to the very recent establishment of a police drug intercepting unit, it is difficult to evaluate the size and number of seizures. Generally, however, the quantities seized have been minimal, with a notable exception. On 27 September 2002 UNMIK Police seized a shipment of 600 kg of marijuana, with an estimated value of US $2 million in the Albanian-populated south Mitrovica (*OSCE/OMIK Monitor* 30 September, 2002; *RFE/RL Newsline* 30 September, 2002). Another large shipment (80 kg of hashish) was seized by Macedonian authorities on 29 March 2002 on its way out of Kosovo, after having already passed KFOR and customs controls. Most drug interceptions, however, are considerably smaller and tend to be concentrated in the Pristina, Gjilan/Gnjilane and Prizren areas (author's interviews with international drug investigators, March and April 2002). From August 2001 to March 2002 the DTU made 155 seizures, of which 60 involved marijuana/cannabis, 38 heroin and 12 hashish (statistics courtesy of the DTU).

The Serb-populated North Mitrovica, which was until November 2002 still controlled by Serb paramilitaries in the service of Belgrade, has had proportionately fewer seizures. This is because CIVPOL had limited access and operability in the Serbian part of the divided town. For example, despite serious suspicion of cannabis plantations, investigators have failed to find substantiating evidence (author's interviews with drug investigators, April 2002). Moreover, after a violent Serb attack against international police on 8 April 2002, UNMIK temporarily abandoned the north, which made it impossible for drug investigators to operate there. While CIVPOL presence gradually trickled back in the months following the attack, it was only in November 2002 that UNMIK formally asserted its authority over the North, with Belgrade's grudging support, and occasional attacks on international police still continue.[13]

In addition, the legislation pertaining to drug trafficking is inadequate. Since the UN assumed the administration of the province in 1999, the applicable law is constituted by regulations promulgated by the UN special representative of the secretary general (SRSG). Where such regulations are lacking, the older Yugoslav legal statutes apply. The UNMIK chief, Michael Steiner, recently signed the new Criminal Code and Criminal Procedure Code on 7 July 2003, an endeavour which took four years of deliberation, and which will take almost another year to enter into force (*RFE/RL Newsline*, 7 July 2003). On the issue of drugs, the only applicable law thus remains article 245 of the old Federal Yugoslav Criminal Code, which makes trade or manufacture of drugs punishable by prison terms between six months and ten years, and does not treat possession or purchase of drugs for personal use as a criminal offence. In other words, when a drug seizure is reported, individuals can only be prosecuted for attempted sale or production.[14]

Trafficking in People and Prostitution

While Kosovo has long been a major transit route for trafficked persons, it is increasingly turning into a final destination (UNICEF/UNOHCHR/OSCE 2002). The majority of trafficked human beings end up in prostitution. Since the UN administration in Kosovo was established, the organization primarily engaged in intercepting human trafficking is the International Organization for Migration (IOM), which is assisted by the Organization for Security and Cooperation in Europe (OSCE) and by the Trafficking and Prostitution Investigation Unit (TPIU) of UNMIK Police, established in October 2000. Between February 2000 and April 2002 the IOM recovered 303 women illegally smuggled and detained in Kosovo brothels. The victims were smuggled primarily from Moldova (52 per cent), Romania (23 per cent), and Ukraine (13 per cent) (IOM 2002). The number of women smuggled across multiple borders into Kosovo points to the multinational nature of organized crime.

Due to the very traditional and closely-knit society in Kosovo, local women who are victims of trafficking are usually not forced into prostitution there, but are instead smuggled abroad, mostly to western Europe, where Albanian criminal groups run extensive prostitution networks. However, as of late there has been evidence that deteriorating social conditions might have changed that trend. The IOM has assisted eight local women trafficked within the province (IOM 2002).[15] To support victims recovered during police raids, the IOM established a temporary shelter where foreign women receive legal, medical and psychological counselling in their own language. The IOM is also charged with organizing repatriation and reintegration in countries of origin, normally after two to three weeks. However, the problem of providing reasonable security against their smugglers, who, according to all evidence, move easily cross borders, is not adequately addressed (author's interviews with the IOM, March 2002). In addition, the professional integrity of some IOM employees in Kosovo can also be questioned since at times they appeared to favor prostitution, rather than work against it (author's interviews with police investigators, September 2002).

UNMIK Regulation 2001/4, 'On the Prohibition of Trafficking in Persons in Kosovo', was adopted in January 2001. It criminalizes trafficking in human beings and provides safeguards for victims, such as temporary shelter and legal, medical and psychological counselling in the victim's native language. Those found guilty of trafficking receive prison terms of two to 20 years, and the property where the offence was committed is confiscated.

While only 10 to 30 per cent of the brothel clientele is international,[16] the highly paid UN, KFOR and international NGO staff present in Kosovo push up prices and keep the business profitable. Some sources have suggested that international police and KFOR might have even been implicated in running prostitution businesses in Kosovo, although there has been no official corroboration to that effect so far (author's interviews with police investigators, September 2002). Ten international police officers have been repatriated for using services of prostitutes. The real number of those implicated in prostitution is suspected to be higher (author's interviews with senior investigative staff, October and November 2002).

As of March 2002, the TPIU had identified 110 suspect establishments – with the highest concentration in the Prizren area. The police closed 55 brothels in 2001, but many re-opened under different names. TPIU updates an off-limits list monthly and distributes it to all UN and KFOR staff in an effort to limit their contribution to the proceeds of organized crime. There are severe disciplinary repercussions for members of the international staff caught during police raids in these establishments. However, these measures are generally only limited to UN and KFOR staff—not to the employees of the numerous NGOs present on the ground. In addition, prostitution services are increasingly offered in private homes upon phone call requests, a fact which makes the adequate interception of trafficking even more difficult (author's interviews, July–September 2002).

From the beginning of 2001 to April 2002, 68 arrests of local offenders on charges of human trafficking were made, resulting in at least 16 convictions. However, collection of evidence is slow and cumbersome, and, due to a highly imperfect legal system, which has taken some highlights from European civil law, evidence gathered by police is not legally admissible in courts. Many trafficked women recovered during police raids are unwilling to testify against their captors, not only in court, but also before investigative judges and IOM/OCSE. Given a very weak witness protection program,[17] they are often too intimidated and not sufficiently protected. This lack of witness testimony – often the only evidence available – seriously undermines prosecution.[18] A small percentage of victims refuse to be repatriated because they lack alternatives at home or fear revenge from traffickers.

Refusal to cooperate with authorities more often than not effectively excludes the woman from being categorized as a victim. It may also preclude her from receiving any assistance and even risk her indictment for prostitution and/or illegal entry into Kosovo, which can result in detention of up to 20 days (author's interview with IOM, March 2002). Such charges should be excluded by the UNMIK Regulation on Trafficking, which prohibits prosecution of victims, but decisions are at the discretion of local judges, whose attitude is rather conservative, and tends to reflect traditional social norms where women are a priori held responsible with little or no regard for the evidence.

To address the needs of victims of trafficking as well as other crimes, UNMIK has set up a Victim Advocacy and Assistance Unit in the Department of Justice, which also has established a referral centre with a 24-hour hotline for all victims of violence. The Victim Assistance Coordinator,[19] a Kosovo official appointed by the special representative of the SRSG, assists the victims with legal advice, and ensures that they receive medical assistance. Given the risk that victims could be charged with prostitution, the coordinator has an important advisory role to play with prosecutors.

Money Laundering and Corruption

Since December 2000, individual commercial bank deposits have grown from US $20,000,000 to US $270,000,000 while those of corporations and other legal entities have risen from US $40,000,000 to US $152,000,000.[20] The exponential growth has increased sensitivity to the risks of money laundering and related forms of corruption, though it is difficult to pinpoint accounts associated with organized crime.

Specific legislation on money laundering and corruption is so far limited to the UNMIK Regulation on Organized Crime, which does not specify that money laundering is an offence. All banks and financial institutions are required to report transactions over US $15,000 to the Banking and Payments Authority of Kosovo (BPK).[21] These reports are handed to the Central Intelligence Unit (CIU) of CIVPOL for investigation. However, there are no requirements to register large sums of money when leaving Kosovo, which creates ample opportunity to launder organized crime money elsewhere in the region. Draft legislation to criminalize money laundering has been under review by the Office of the Legal Advisor (OLA) for at least a year, but a formal regulation on the subject is still missing (Author's interviews with BPK officials, April 2002).

The agenda of the Kosovo government includes anti-corruption measures within the draft laws on procurement, conflict of interest, conduct of public servants and freedom of information. The PISG have also requested that major international donors assist it in establishing anti-corruption strategies, but recent arrests on corruption charges, which will be discussed below, indicate that the phenomenon is pervasive.

The lack of legislation on money laundering and corruption creates numerous possibilities to engage in both activities. While it is suspected that money is being laundered through financial institutions as well as dubious lottery establishments (Qirezi 2002), there is also a risk that donor money might be channelled into organized crime. Most major donors perform risk assessments and frequent audits. However, inquiries into local aid recipients or tender winners are laborious. Despite the donor auditing mechanisms, weak institutions at both central and municipal levels, imperfect local accounting mechanisms, and the high number of cash transactions facilitate diversion.[22]

In an effort to detect and counter financial fraud, especially in the public domain, in July 2002 the current SRSG Michael Steiner negotiated an agreement with the Italian government which seconded ten experts from the Guardia di Finanza, the Italian specialized Fiscal Police. They began their work in late 2002 in parallel with UNMIK's Financial Inspection Unit, which monitors account transactions in Kosovo. The Guardia di Finanza experts were initially contracted for six months, a less-than-adequate period to conclude complex investigations of financial fraud in a foreign land. During this time they have conducted complex investigations into KEK, the Kosovo's troubled electricity company, provided grounds for the arrest of Leme Xhema, the director of the Kosovo's telephone company PTK, and are also investigating corruption the health sector. There is an on-going controversy over the renewal of the Guardia di Finanza secondment, which the UN would like to continue to be at the expense of the Italian government, while the Italian government would like the UN to pay for it (*OSCE/OMIK Monitor Final edition*, 2 July 2003).

The BPK, with an entirely international staff, is also concerned with background checks on both the financial institutions and their clients. It has broad discretionary licensing and monitoring powers, including denial or removal of licenses, removal of shareholders and senior management, fines, change of an institution's required capital, and the freezing of accounts.[23] It has used virtually all these powers due to the detection of large suspicious transactions on the part of both local and international actors. It has likewise denied bank licenses to eight applicants on suspicion of involvement in money laundering, a fact that strongly points to the wide scope of the problem.[24]

While waiting for legislation, the BPK has prepared detailed Money Laundering Guidance Notes for all registered banks and financial institutions. However, BPK officials admit that it is difficult to check every customer's account movements, especially wired transactions. Moreover, due to its non-sovereign status, Kosovo cannot be a full member of international financial information exchange mechanisms such as the Financial Action Task Force (FATF). One success BPK claims is having attracted in recent months large sums of money floating around Kosovo's informal economy into the banking system, where at least some control can be exercised. Naturally, it is easy to speculate that organized crime in Kosovo tends to avail of foreign banking services where central bank supervision is minimal.

Arms Trafficking

Given the abundance of armed conflict in the Balkans, weapons smuggling through Kosovo has been endemic. The flow of arms, mostly of Soviet or eastern European origin, was first boosted by fighting in the neighbouring areas – in particular, Bosnia and Herzegovina. The breakdown of the Albanian military structure in 1990, and in particular the virtual collapse of state institutions in 1996–1997 during which police and army barracks were looted, also contributed. After the emergence of the Kosovo Liberation Army, the concentration of weapons in the province dramatically increased.[25] Bringing weapons circulation and possession under control is therefore a tremendous task. KFOR and the police are engaged more in weapons containment than in weapons reduction.

UNMIK regulation 2001/7 adopted on February 2001 bans unauthorized possession of weapons by all Kosovo residents. Depending on the gravity of the offence, trade or illegal possession of arms can be punished with a fine of US $7,500 or a prison term of up to eight years. UNMIK instituted two weapons amnesty programs, the latest from 15 March to 15 April 2002, to give residents the opportunity to hand in weapons without punishment. The amnesties have had limited success. In the latest, KPS and the police collected 62,193 items. By contrast, seizures of weapons and ammunition for the same period totaled 361,894 (statistics courtesy of KFOR). On 9 July 2003 a study commissioned by the UNDP and conducted by the Small Arms Survey, estimated that between 330,000 and 460,000 firearms are still believed to be illegally owned by civilians in Kosovo (UNMIK 2003).

KFOR, UNMIK's international police, and the KPS, have all engaged in weapons searches and confiscation, assisted by Kosovo Customs, but weapons flows through the province are abundant.[26] Understaffed and underpaid customs officials are obvious targets for organized crime.[27] Mixed shipments coming out or going into Kosovo are often not broken down in customs declarations, and regular and efficient controls are still very difficult to implement (author's interviews with senior UN procurement officials, May 2002). Weapons seizures mostly occur from an intelligence tips rather than routine customs controls (author's interviews with Carabinieiri at MSU, April and August 2002).

The biggest seizure was made on 14 June 2001 in the Pec/Peje region. A Bosnian-registered truck, which had passed through KFOR and customs controls in the Klina checkpoint on the boundary with Montenegro (allegedly one of the most problematic control points), was seized by the Italian Carabinieri on its way to Macedonia (ibid.).[28] According to the UNMIK police spokesperson, most Kosovo newspapers were reluctant to report the episode because it was believed to be directly linked to the conflict in Macedonia, where the ethnic Albanians are closely related to those in Kosovo (author's interview with Derek Chappell, UMNIK Police spokesperson, September 2002). Based on several similar seizures in the following months, the authorities believe there was a consistent weapons flow during 2001 from Bosnia and Herzegovina, and to a lesser extent from Albania, through Kosovo and into Macedonia. In the spring of 2001, many of these weapons were destined for the armed struggle between the National Liberation Army (NLA) – which was closely linked to the former KLA in Kosovo – and the Macedonian authorities (author's interviews with police and KFOR, April, May, June and September 2002). There has also been an intensification of the activities of another organization believed to be closely related to the former two – the Albanian National Army (AKSH), which was outlawed as a terrorist organization in April 2003 following an attack on a North Mitrovica bridge (*OSCE/OMIK Monitor Final Edition*, 26 June 2003; *UNMIK Police Briefing Notes*, 1 July 2003; *RFE/RL Newsline*, 3 July 2003).

Statistics of seizures in 2002 are not yet sufficient to determine if this weapons flow has subsided with the improvement of security in that country. Officials at KFOR and UNMIK Police believe that many arms designated for Macedonia already reached their destination in 2001, and that few and relatively old pieces of ammunition were turned in or recovered during NATO's operation Essential Harvest. Based on recent seizures, however, KFOR officials say that illegal arms are increasingly being moved toward Montenegro's Mediterranean coast, presumably intended for further sea shipment (author's interviews with KFOR, July, September 2002).[29]

In another worrisome development, two ethnic Albanians (one a Macedonian citizen) were arrested on 12 August 2002 in the process of acquiring a significant quantity of ammunition and assault weapons apparently intended for the so-called Liberation Army of Illiria (*UNMIK Police Press Release*, 4 October 2002; interview with CIVPOL spokesman, October 2002). Due to the extreme objectives of this organization, i.e. the unification within political borders of ethnic Albanians in Macedonia, Kosovo and Albania, and the possibility of its links to terrorist groups, the suspects were detained in Camp Bondsteel, the American military base in Kosovo.

LEGAL AND INSTITUTIONAL PROBLEMS

With its unique mandate, UNMIK has the opportunity, as well as the responsibility, to build both a socio-political framework to discourage organized crime and a strong police and justice system to fight it. However, it still needs to address serious gaps in the current legal framework. In September 2001 UNMIK adopted a regulation specifically pertaining to organized crime. It draws on the UN Convention on Transnational Organized Crime and is rather general in its definition of 'serious crime'.[30] The specific regulations addressing the individual areas discussed above do not appear to be substantively linked to this general regulation.

Key legislation, such as regulations on drug possession and trade, money laundering, and corruption, needs to be streamlined. Without an improved protection program, witnesses will not provide crucial evidence needed for indictments and conviction. While enforcement of the just promulgated July 2003 Criminal Code and Criminal Procedure Code is still almost a year away, speculations regarding its implementation upon enforcement are also pessimistic (author's interviews with UNMIK Police, June 2003).[31]

Kosovo's law enforcement authorities also lack full investigative capacity. Attempts to establish a unified investigative structure are surprisingly recent.[32] For example, while systematic liaison and intelligence sharing between investigative units is fundamental, it was only in late 2001 that UNMIK established a coordinating body under the UNMIK police commissioner: the Kosovo Organised Crime Bureau (KOCB). It is meant to identify, gather evidence against, arrest and prosecute perpetrators of organized crime and to take or recommend adequate countering measures (UNSC 2002). After a half-year during which the KOCB's operational capacity was apparently quite limited due to poor organization and lagging professionalism,[33] it seems finally to be better structured and prepared to fulfil its mandate (author's interviews with KOCB, August 2002).

Three closely related bodies are key to KOCB's ability to gain and analyse intelligence information and weigh the admissibility of evidence for court use, namely the UNMIK Police CIU, the CCIU, and the Sensitive Information and Operations Unit (SIOU) of the Department of Justice. However, given their often overlapping functions and competencies, the question of duplication of activity at the expense of efficiency naturally arises. The KOCB recently submitted to the UNMIK police commissioner a report which identifies major difficulties the body is still facing in performing its duties. Some of these include the high turnover of police investigators and the clumsiness of the legal system when authorizing covert operations or issuing court orders (author's interviews with KOCB, November 2002; *UNMIK Police Annual Report*, 5 December 2002). Finally, even if the UN eventually disposes of an independent institution specifically tailored to the fight against organized crime, insiders report that crucial to the efficient functioning of that unit is the personal relationship between the head of the KOCB and the UNMIK police commissioner, which, if contrasting, appears to seriously undermine the efficiency of the entire system (author's interviews with KOCB, November 2002).

Performance of thorough background security checks on local employees is an additional problem, as is the fact that UNMIK Police continue to rely on local intelligence tips, while struggling with language barriers and an unfamiliar environment.[34] These circumstances make the participation of local KPS officers crucial to successful operations. However, several factors undermine the capacity and credibility of the KPS: they require further training in modern policing methods; they are not yet fully operational in crucial areas such as North Mitrovica; multi-ethnic patrols are still limited, and some officers retain links to the former KLA.[35]

The strong regional linkages of criminal networks, the Balkans' notoriously porous borders, widespread corruption among local customs officials, and the relatively weak institutional capacities of the neighbouring Balkan countries to fight crime further complicate Kosovo's internal difficulties. Problems are also created by the lack of a coherent and comprehensive regional organized crime database or information exchange, by the limited operational capacities, and by the absence of general coordination among the major regional organizations engaged in fighting organized crime.[36]

THE IMPACT ON SOCIETY AND POLITICS

Without factoring in the deterrent effect organized criminal activities have on potential outside investment, it is obvious that organised crime has a seriously effect on Kosovo's formal economy. For example, Kosovo loses an estimated US $18 million each year from cigarette smuggling alone, mainly in excise tax evasion (*RFE/RL Newsline*, 13 May 2002), though this apparently represents a decrease because of tightened customs controls.[37] Fifty per cent of all fuel in Kosovo is smuggled into the province (A. Kelmendi 2002), particularly through problematic border crossings such as those with Montenegro, where pipes for smuggling it are quite evident.[38] A March 2003 investigation in the wake of the arrest of a high-profile Prizren Registration Centre official revealed that of the 247 private vehicles checked, the documentation of 178 legally registered ones was fraudulent (*UNMIK Police Press Release*, 5 March 2003). Occasional search operations still reveal a rampant market for stolen vehicles 'from all over Europe' (*UNMIK Police Briefing Notes*, 1 July 2003).

Although authoritative Kosovo-specific research has not yet been done into the impact of organized crime on society and politics, examples in other European post-Communist societies suggest that it is likely to be significant. Corruption linked to organized crime, for example, has contributed importantly to the serious erosion of Macedonia's internal security and stability (Dao 2002). The pervasiveness of organized crime has diminished Russian economic development by radically restricting the tax base, discouraging foreign investment, and enabling capital flight (Shelly 1997). In addition, social scientists point out that organized crime has led to a virtual breakdown in norms and values in the Russian society, where it has apparently become acceptable, and perhaps even expected, for business and political leaders to engage in illegal activities for personal benefit (Frisby 1998).

Given the statistics just cited, which are only the tip of the iceberg, it is unclear whether UNMIK has been able to contain the infiltration of organized crime into Kosovo's government institutions. Moreover, the period of maximum vulnerability probably lies immediately ahead, as the UN proceeds to transfer authority to the new PISG at the provincial and municipal levels where institutions continue to be weak.

The September 2002 arrest of two senior administrators in the course of investigation of the activities of the former KLA commander Rrustem Mustafa (Remi) and others may provide a glimpse into the links between organized crime and politics in the province.[39] According to UNMIK Police spokespersons, the arrested officials were connected to one of the most influential political parties in Kosovo, the PDK, the province's second largest party, some of whose members are among the primary suspects in the continuing investigation (author's interviews with UNMIK CIVPOL spokespersons Derek Chappell and Barry Fletcher, September, 2002; see also *OSCE/OMIK Monitor Final Edition*, 26 September 2002). It is also suspected that prominent political personalities benefited from the illegal transfers of municipality land to private individuals over a period of two-and-a-half years in a giant fraud operation that makes 80 per cent of the registered total of 15,000 property transfers questionable (*OSCE/OMIK Monitor Final Edition*). The Pristina municipality is now run by LDK, Kosovo's President Rugova's party, but until October 2000, it was controlled by the PDK. However, the illegal transfers were clearly unaffected by the party in charge of the municipality, continuing well until the arrest of the suspects.

TACKLING ORGANIZED CRIME

To achieve the international community's objectives in ensuring Kosovo's peaceful political and economic development, more progress in the fight against organized crime is essential. That requires the strengthening of the institutions and the filling of legal and operational gaps. Failure to do so, and sooner rather than later in the process of turning over responsibilities to local authorities, will seriously impair the province's stability and democratic transition, and make it a haven for international criminality and terrorism.

UNMIK's experience so far suggests that further steps to strengthen its capacity to counter organized crime are needed. While the inauguration, on 7 July 2003, of a new Criminal Code and a new Criminal Procedure Code, after four years of deliberation, is an important improvement in producing a unified body of law for Kosovo, implementation of the new statute is likely to remain problematic. Further streamlining of the procedures regarding money laundering and on possession, manufacture and trade of and in drugs is needed. A comprehensive victim protection program should be enacted.

Another important area for improvement has to do with the selection, training and integration of KPS officers, whose cooperation and professionalism are crucial. Language skills, basic investigative training, adequate salaries and genuine commitment are qualities that need to be promoted through sustained specialized education and the opportunity to learn the experiences of other countries. Building trust in and legitimacy of the local police will require frequent professional consultation and exchange, as well as the gradual delegation of increased responsibility. Efforts until now have been rather limited in both time and scope.

Cooperation with international organized crime registries and organizations outside Kosovo, including Interpol, Europol and the various regional organizations with related objectives and capabilities, has been very sporadic and limited, partly because of Kosovo's unresolved status.[40] Agreements should be negotiated to make such cooperation routine. Given the multi-ethnic and international nature of organized crime, coordination should be considerably improved both between intelligence-gathering bodies within Kosovo and between Kosovo and the rest of the Balkan region. A regional policing database, professional standardization and common arrest mandates should be instituted.[41]

A final consideration worth mentioning is the linkage between the problems related to Kosovo's undetermined final status and their impact on organized crime. Kosovo's leaders have repeatedly claimed that an international recognition of Kosovo as an independent state would have a positive impact on the efforts for combating organized crime in the province, as well as contribute to the stabilization of the overall security situation in the region.[42] Local police officers are increasingly reluctant to report to foreign commanders, aspiring for more autonomy and freedom of action (Green 2003). Independence is considered a panacea for all problems plaguing the province (Bardos 2002), and the failure of the international community to deliver on that front—the basis for renewed war scenarios (Moore 2003).

While the prospect of Kosovo's final status resolution and its impact on regional security has been addressed in depth elsewhere (Stefanova 2003), it needs to be noted that a recognition of independent Kosovo within the next three to four years, will not, in all likelihood, contribute to the efforts for tackling organized crime in the province. As is evident from the preceding discussion, the transfer of authority has proven particularly laborious, not only because of institutional inefficiencies typical of the UN bureaucracy, but also, and above all, because of societal idiosyncrasies, which make Kosovo's institutions particularly vulnerable to manipulations by criminal interests. As noted by Colonel Mike Hoffpauir, the US Army's chief civil affairs officer in Kosovo, organized crime has an influence at both the central and the municipal level in the province, and local police officers continue to be vulnerable to mafia pressures (Green 2003). Many observers believe that the local authorities' commitment to the rule of law remains inadequate, and that independence will not contribute to its consolidation, but will, conversely, make Kosovo's fledgling institutions more susceptible to organized crime interests.[43] As a result, despite its own institutional inefficiencies described earlier in this survey, the UN today remains more committed and better equipped to tackling organized crime in Kosovo than the local leadership. This consideration points to both a unique opportunity and a heavy responsibility the UN has to stop the pernicious influence of organized crime from impacting the province's political, economic and social development. In view of the well-networked and far-reaching capacity of Kosovo organized crime, a procrastination in strengthening the UN mechanisms to tackle this problem will not only seriously impair Kosovo's future, but is also likely to undermine regional stability in the Balkans.

ACKNOWLEDGEMENTS

This research is an elaboration of a series of interviews conducted by the author in Kosovo between March and November 2002. The views expressed in this article are solely the author's. They do not represent the official position of either the publisher or the author's current or previous employers.

NOTES

1. It is worth noting that besides the charities, which are mostly linked to Saudi Arabia, there are also businesses from Middle Eastern countries, notably Jordan and Egypt, whose presence in Kosovo is disproportional, given the virtual lack of economic productivity in Kosovo. For example, when asked how he decided to open a restaurant in Pristina, a Jordanian national replied that he first visited Kosovo for tourism in 2000 and decided that was a good location. It should be noted that Kosovo is by no stretch of the imagination a 'tourist location'. Author's interview, July 2002.
2. In an editorial commentary speculating about the killing of one of the former Kosovo military commanders, Tahir Zemaj, widely suspected of involvement in organized crime, on 4 January 2003, Vetton Surroi, the well-known and respected editor of Kosovo's most influential daily newspaper, *Koha Ditore* stated that 'the one who pulls the trigger is not important. It is the whole political system, which created a mechanism through which crime and politics could live together, by enriching each other' (*Koha Dittore*, 6 January 2003).
3. The relevant benchmark goal reads 'Organised crime networks disrupted, financial crime checked, and end of extremist violence' (UNMIK's 'Standards Before Status', endorsed Senior Representative of the Secretary General (SRSG) Michael Steiner in May 2002).
4. The bulk of the KLA's own funding was generated mainly through the drug trade. The KLA also instituted a special fund named 'Homeland Calling', where substantial donations from the Albanian diasporas in western Europe and the United States were gathered (Sullivan 1998).
5. The centres for organized crime dominated by Kosovo Albanians are Pristina and Prizren in Kosovo, Veliki Trnovac and Blastica in Serbia, Gostivar, Vratnica and Skopje in Macdonia, and Tirana, Durres and Shkoder in Albania (Milivojevic 1995; Prentice 1999; Seper 1999).
6. Author interviews with UNMIK international prosecutors and investigators, March–August, 2002. See also Fleishman (1999). In 1994 as much as 70 per cent of the heroin traffic to Switzerland was said to be controlled by Albanians from Kosovo or Albania (*Guardian* 1994). The same figure is also cited by Judah (1994).
7. Author's periodical interviews with international investigators and prosecutors, March–November 2002. Also to be noted is Chief Prosecutor for the International Tribunal for the Former Yugoslavia Carla del Ponte's statement that she finds it difficult to issue

indictments as witnesses are too afraid to testify (*RFE/RL Newsline*, 22 November 2002). For example, on 13 December 2003 a key witness testifying in the Remi Mustafa (a KLA commander) trial was injured in an explosion in Pristina. On 15 April, Ilir Selimaj, a key witness in a high-profile trial against the so-called Dukagjini Group, suspected also of involvement in organized crime, was killed with other members of his family on 14 April 2003 (*OSCE/OMIK Monitor Final Edition*, 15 April 2003).

8. As early as 1985 *The Wall Street Journal* reported a strong 'Balkan connection' for a growing number of criminal activities on US territory (9 September 1985).

9. Kosovo, with a population of about 2 million, receives more aid per capita than any of the other countries in the region.

10. Interview with Special Representative of the Secretary General Michael Steiner on CNN's Q&A, 31 July 2002. See also Steiner's 11 March 2002 statement to the NATO Secretary General, Lord Robertson, outlining that the fight against organized crime is the next priority of the international administration in Kosovo (*Monitor Morning News Digest*, 12 March 2002). On 11 April 2002, when commenting on the expected reorganization of KFOR troops, COMKFOR Marcel Valentin underlined that over the next six months KFOR will be primarily concerned with fighting organized crime (radio interviews, as reported by the *Daily Broadcast Media Monitor*, 12 April 2002).

11. Some indictments for organized crime have been linked to war crimes (author's interviews with international prosecutors, April and June 2002).

12. The leaves and stalks of the cannabis plant are used for production of both marijuana and hashish. The latter is a less sophisticated product, easier to produce and cheaper. For these reasons, it is more commonly consumed in Kosovo and the Balkans generally than marijuana, which is primarily exported to western Europe.

13. The latest Serb attack on a joint CIVPOL/KPS operation was carried out on 18 July 2003 (UNMIK press release, 18 July 2003). It should be noted that international police are also routinely attacked in Albanian-populated areas: hand grenades were thrown at CIVPOL stations in Podujevo and Pristina on 17 and 21 July respectively after the Prisitina district court concluded the Remi trial on 16 July with a long-term prison sentence for the former KLA *commanders (OSCE/OMIK Monitor Final Edition*, 18 and 21 July 2003). Police stations in Pristina were also attacked on 21 March.

14. Within the Yugoslav Criminal Code, a Law on Minor Offences does provide for up to a week's detention for drug possession. However, UNMIK investigators have avoided using such detention as they hope suspects can be persuaded to be helpful in uncovering larger transactions (uthor's interviews with international prosecutors, August 2002).

15. NGOs in Kosovo providing shelter for victims of domestic violence have also commented on the increase in 'internally' trafficked women – Kosovo women forced into prostitution.

16. This figure differed considerably depending on the source: the TPIU stated that the international clientele is 8 to 10 per cent; the OSCE and the IOM put it at 30 per cent (author's interviews, March 2002). The UNICEF/UNOHCHR/OSCE – ODIHR June 2002 Report indicated that the percentage was as high as 40 per cent, of which the majority were reportedly KFOR soldiers (p.96).

17. Most countries have refused to accommodate witnesses from Kosovo, where it is practically impossible for them to be adequately protected.

18. The UNMIK Judicial Development Division has recently set up a Victim Advocacy and Assistance Unit, which will initially be sponsored by the OSCE. The operability of this body remains to be tested.

19. Such a position was foreseen in UNMIK Regulation 2001/4, 'On the Prohibition of Trafficking in Persons in Kosovo', 12 January 2001.

20. *BPK Monthly Statistics Bulletin*, No.2, March 2002, p.9. The increase in deposits was in part induced by the conversion to the euro.

21. Section 22 of UNMIK Regulation 1999/21, 'Bank Licensing, Supervision, and Regulation', and Rule X of the Banking and Payments Authority of Kosovo (BPK) outline reporting requirements of banks in Kosovo. This is the same amount that customs asks arrivals in Kosovo to declare.

22. Author's interviews with donors, March 2002. It is worth noting in this respect the illegal transfer of US $4.5 million by a senior UNMIK official from Germany from the budget of the Kosovo Energy Company (KEK) to an offshore account, announced by UNMIK on 30 April 2002. It was not until late November 2002 that the offender was arrested (author's interviews with police investigators, April and May 2002).
23. See UNMIK Regulation No.1999/21, 'On Bank Licensing, Supervision, and Regulation', 15 November 1999.
24. At least one of those applicants was from Luxembourg, a noted tax haven in Europe. There are currently seven licensed baking institutions in Kosovo (author's interviews with BPK officials, April 2002).
25. Judah (1994) suggests that preparations for an armed struggle in Kosovo, a process during which the Kosovo fighters were arming using drug money in exchange for weapons and ammunition, were underway before the actual emergence of the KLA. See also Drozdiak (1993a,b) and Viviano (1994).
26. For example, since January 2003, UNMIK launched a 'Zero Tolerance Against Illegal Weapons' campaign, instituting numerous checkpoints and performing random searches of individuals, cars and houses. Only over six days in early February 2003, 119 illegal weapons were recovered (UNMIK Police press release, 5 February 2003). It is worth noting that customs officials do not perform patrols (author's interviews with customs officials, April and September 2002).
27. Kosovo Customs Director Ylber Raci was arrested by UNMIK Police on 17 May 2002 on charges of corruption and abuse of office, following a two-year investigation (*RFE/RL Newsline*, 20 May 2002). Raci was later released, however, for lack of evidence.
28. It carried heavy ammunition, notably six anti-aircraft missiles, 97 anti-tank missiles, four mortars, 451 hand grenades and explosives, 466 light weapons and 44,966 other pieces of combat ammunition. Statistics courtesy of Carabinieri and Italian KFOR.
29. UNMIK and KFOR officials say they do not know the ultimate destinations of such shipments, even if many speculate shipments to North Africa and the Middle East. A joint KFOR/CIVPOL operation, which started in early June 2002 has recovered by October 2002 eight air defence weapons, 207 rockets/missiles, 1,182 anti-tank weapons, 91 support weapons, 931 pistols, 2 433 rifles (mostly AK-47s), 4,456 grenades/mines, and 459,808 other items of combat ammunition. Statistics courtesy of Carabinieri and Italian KFOR.
30. See UNMIK Regulation No.2001/22 'On Measures Against Organised Crime', 20 September 2001. The regulation's preamble mentions the desire to be consistent with the Convention on Transnational Organised Crime (CTOC) adopted by the UN General Assembly in December 2000. The convention emphasises the economic manifestations of organized crime (in particular, money laundering and corruption), while crimes related to people trafficking and weapons smuggling – issues of utmost relevance in Kosovo – are addressed in three optional protocols not specifically referred to in UNMIK's regulation. While the convention still needs to be ratified, it is the only UN instrument in the field of organized crime. The regulation does not incorporate the convention by reference. Kosovo must await specific regulations in areas such as money laundering, which are now being drafted (author's interviews with international prosecutors, May–July 2002).
31. It was specifically pointed out that some resistance to efficient implementation procedures for the new code was also to be found in the Kosovo Assembly.
32. For example, it was only in 2002 that UNMIK Police received a mandate to conduct undercover or covert operations during investigations. Even now, they have to go through an elaborate authorisation procedure that impedes efficiency. In addition, intelligence sharing between CIVPOL and KFOR has apparently not been as forthcoming as needed (author's interviews with police, August 2002).
33. An insider from UNMIK interviewed by the author in August 2002, questioned the operational capacity of the KOCB.
34. Currently UNMIK Police, in particular the US CIVPOL, are discouraged from speaking the local languages in an effort to appear neutral. This rather controversial policy,

however, impedes efficient intelligence gathering by requiring reliance on third parties (interpreters, assistants, etc.) (author's interviews with UNMIK Police, August 2002).

35. The first KPS Police Academy was launched in December 1999. It was agreed by UNMIK that at least 50 per cent of students would be former KLA fighters. The actual percentage is believed to be about 60 per cent. Clearly ethnic Albanian KPS officers are thus a priori compromised in the eyes of the Serbian population. Managing to recruit Serbian KPS officers, on the other hand, has proved particularly difficult, since Serbs often to boycott or reluctantly participate in Kosovo's institutions (author's interviews with UNMIK Police, July and August 2002, and with Serb political leaders, April, 2002).

36. Prime among these is the Stability Pact for South-East Europe, whose Table 3, dealing with security issues, specifically addresses organized crime (under the sub-table on Justice and Home Affairs). In October 2000, the Stability Pact launched a multi-targeted 'Initiative Against Organized Crime in South-East Europe (SPOC)', whose objective was, among other things, to create a regional database for organized crime. A special project on the 'Contribution of Exchange of Information Systems to the Fight Against Organized Crime in the South-East Europe Countries' was launched within that framework, that aims to link the regional database (once it is established) to Interpol, Europol and the Schengen Information System, but no concrete results have yet ensued, as of the time of writing. In addition, an Advisory and Contact Group, where the other major organizations dealing with organized crime also have a seat, was established in an effort aimed at better coordination, but the operational capacity of that body still needs to be tested. The Southeastern Europe Cooperation Initiative (SECI), which benefits from the expertise of an FBI advisory committee, also aims at establishing a regional organized crime database, which is still to be completed, reportedly by the end of 2002. However, the SECI common database project covers only trafficking of human beings, even if the organization also deals with other aspects of organized crime. UNMIK Police officials claim that preliminary cooperation within that framework has been very useful for their work in Kosovo. (author's interviews, October 2002). Other regional initiatives dealing with organized crime also include the Adriatic Sea Initiative, the Balkans Foreign and Defense Ministerials, and the Central European Initiative (CEI).

37. *UNMIK News*, 6 May, available at ⟨http://www.unmikonline.org/new.htm⟩. UNMIK decided to host a regional forum to counter cigarette smuggling in the Balkans on 10 May 2002, stressing that the problem can only be adequately addressed on a regional basis.

38. During an author's trip to the Kosovo–Montenegro boundary in June 2002 she noticed and photographed pipes, garden hoses, tankers, pumps, several trucks without license plates, and as many as seven gas stations in the 5-km ground safety zone between Kosovo and Montenegro. See also I. Kelmendi (2002); on a speculation of the profits from illegal transfers of oil, see also *RFE/RL Newsline*, 9 July 2003.

39. The Pristina Director of Cadastre, Geodesy and Property, Sharr Pllana, and his senior assistant, Avdullah Demolli, were arrested on charges of aggravated corruption and fraud. UNMIK Police Press Release, 24 September 2002; OSCE/OMIK Monitor final edition, 25 September 2002; *RFE/RL Newsline*, vol. 6, No. 181, part II, 25 September 2002. Demolli was temporarily released while awaiting trial, based on a decision of an international investigating judge.

40. For this reason UNMIK Police access to the Interpol database was effectively precluded until an Interpol office was recently opened in Belgrade. On 31 May 2002 UNMIK and the Belgrade authorities signed a Protocol on Police Cooperation. However, Interpol has reportedly been very slow in providing requested information to the Kosovo institutions dealing with organized crime, which prefer direct resort to individual governments (author's interviews, June–August 2002).

41. UNMIK has proposed a regional equivalent of Interpol, as an improvement on the current fragmented and often duplicative initiatives pertaining to organised crime in southeast Europe (author's discussions with UNMIK spokespersons Derek Chapel and Barry Fletcher, May 2002). Similar conclusions are advanced by Davis, Hirst and Mariani (2001: 66–7).

42. Assembly of Kosovo Declaration on Security of 23 January 2003, as quoted in the *OSCE ASI Newsletter*, March 2003, p. 11.
43. Testimony of Janet Bogue, deputy assistant secretary for South Central Europe, before the US House of Representatives' International Relations Committee, Washington, DC, 21 May 2003; Bardos (2002).

REFERENCES

Bardos, Gordon N. (2002): 'Kosovo Needs a Talking-To', *The Washington Post*, 23 August, p.A27.

Bovenkerk, Frank (2001): 'Organised Crime and Ethnic Minorities: Is there a Link?', *Transnational Organised Crime*, 4:3–4.

Chazan, Yigal (1994): 'Albanian Mafias Find New Drug Routes around Yugoslavia', *Christian Science Monitor*, 20 October 1994, p.6.

Dao, James (2002): 'U.S. and Allies Must Increase Aid to Balkans, a Panel Asserts', *The New York Times*, 9 December.

Davis, Ian, Chrissie Hirst and Bernardo Mariani (2001): *Organised Crime, Corruption and Illicit Arms Trafficking in an Enlarged EU*. London: SaferWorld.

Drozdiak, William (1993a): 'Balkan War Victor: Heroin: New Routes Convey Drugs across Europe', *The Washington Post*, 6 November, p.A1.

Drozdiak, William (1993b): 'Merchants of Death and Drugs: Porous Borders, Balkan War Bring Epidemics of Heroin Smuggling, Arms Sales', *The Houston Chronicle*, 14 November.

Economist (2002): 'Thankless Tasks', *The Economist*, 31 August, p.22.

Fleishman, Jeffrey (1999): "Italy Battling a New Wave of Criminals – Albanians: Refugees are Cutting into the Mafia Turf", *The Philadelphia Inquirer*, 15 March.

Frisby, Tanya (1998): 'The Rise of Organised Crime in Russia: Its Roots and Social Significance', *Europe-Asia Studies*, January.

Green, Peter S. (2003): 'Kosovo Force Takes a Bite Out of Crime', *International Herald Tribune*, 19 May.

Guardian (1994): 'Albanian Drug Barons Find Their Way Around The War', *The Guardian*, 1 November, p.12

IOM (2002): *Return and Reintegration Project Situation Report, February 2000-April 2002*. Kosovo: International Organization on Migration.

Judah, Tim (1994): 'Albanian Mafias Target Drug Routes', *The Times*, 18 October.

Kelmendi, Adriatik (2002): 'Kosovo: Fuel Smuggling Flourishing', *Balkan Crisis Report*, No.321, 28 February.

Kelmendi, Ibrahim (2002): 'Në Zonë Neutrale Zhvillohet Një Kontrabandë Shumë Profesionale Dhe Krejt Legale', *Koha Ditore*, 23 July, p.7.

Layne, Ken (1999): 'The Crime Syndicate Behind the KLA', *MoJo Wire*, 8 April, available at ⟨http://www.motherjones.com/total_coverage/kosovo/layne2.html⟩.

Milivojevic, Marko (19950: 'The Balkan Medellin', *Jane's Intelligence Review*, 7:2, pp.68–9.

Moore, Patrick (2003): 'Three War Scenarios for Kosova', *RFE/RL Balkan Report*, 7:41.

Paoli, Letizia (2001): 'Criminal Fraternities or Criminal Enterprises?', *Transnational Organised Crime*, 4:3–4.

Phillips, David L. (2002): 'Rule of Law: Keeping the Balkans Free of Al Qaeda', *The Wall Street Journal*, 13 February.

Politi, Allesandro (1999): 'The New Dimensions of Organized Crime in Southeastern Europe', *The International Spectator*, 34:4, pp.49–59.

Prentice, Eve-Ann (1999): 'Kosovo is Mafia's Heroin Gateway to West', *The Times*, 24 July.

Qirezi, Arben (2002): 'Kosovo: Lottery Arrests Highlight Growth in Fraud', *Balkan Crisis Report*, No.328.

Seper, Jerry (1999): 'KLA Finances Fight with Heroin Sales', *The Washington Times*, 3 May, p.1.
Shelly, Louise I. (1997): 'The Price Tag of Russia's Organised Crime', *Transition Newsletter*, 8:1.
Stefanova, Radoslava (2003): 'New Security Challenges in the Balkans', *Security Dialogue*, 34:2, pp.169–82.
Sullivan, Stacy (1998): 'Albanian Americans Funding Rebels' Cause', *The Washington Post*, 26 May, p.A12.
Times (1999): 'Drugs Money Linked to Kosovo Rebels', *The Times*, 24 March.
UNICEF/UNOHCHR/OSCE–ODIHR (2002): *Trafficking in Human Beings in South-Eastern Europe*. Belgrade: UNICEF.
UNMIK (2003): *Kosovo and the Gun, A Baseline Assessment of Small Arms and Light Weapons in Kosovo*, UN Interim Mission in Kosovo, available at ⟨http://www.unmikonline.org/archives/news07_03full.htm#0907⟩.
UNSC (2002): *Report of the Secretary General on the United Nations Interim Administration Mission in Kosovo*, S/2002/62. New York: UN Security Council.
Viviano, Frank (1994): 'Drugs Paying for Conflict in Europe: Separatists Supporting Themselves With Traffic in Narcotics', *The San Francisco Chronicle*, 10 June.

Fighting Transborder Organized Crime in Southeast Europe through Fighting Corruption in Customs Agencies

EMI VELKOVA, SASO GEORGIEVSKI

INTRODUCTION

In the past 12 years, transborder organized crime and corruption, the result to a large extent of inefficient state institutions and weak implementation of the law, have continually plagued the countries of southeast Europe (SEE). Both trends have been identified by the European Union (EU) as major problems in SEE countries and obstacles to their European integration. Naturally, the EU is concerned about the presence of organized crime and corruption in SEE, because the EU system expects the courts and public administration of member states to implement, observe and enforce community law. In fact, the effective fight against corruption has become a crucial criterion for the EU for the assessment of the progress made by SEE countries within the context of the Stabilization and Association Process.

According to the EU criteria, a criminal group has a characteristic of organized crime if it has cooperative structure of more than two persons for a long or indefinite period of time, and conducts serious crimes with a purpose of gaining profit and/or power (Viano 1999: 13–21).[1]

The collapse of the Soviet Union and of the Communist regimes in central and eastern Europe and the integration process in the EU have favoured transnational organized crime. More specifically, the promotion in the EU of free movement of goods, services and people has provided criminal organizations with broader scope to expand their businesses and to invest and profit through such practices.

The sanctions and embargo imposed on the Federal Republic of Yugoslavia led to proliferation of organized crime and especially of smuggling, human trafficking and illegal trade, and fostered the development of a regional net of smuggling channels with organized crime structures in Bulgaria, Romania and Albania. On the other hand, rising unemployment and a rising discrepancy between wages and prices pushed many people into the grey economy and on to the black market.

The geographic position of southeast Europe favours organized crime, both transnational and national, leading to illegal trafficking and customs corruption.[2] The Balkans region is a crossroads of international routes and exchanges that link the West to the East and the South to the North. It is the crossroads of the main Pan-European Corridors (Corridor 8 and Corridor 10) and create opportunities for organized crime at transnational and regional levels.

Close connection exists between transborder organized crime and corruption. Corruption does not need organized crime to flourish. However, where there is organized crime there is also corruption, and transborder crime depends on corruption among customs and migration officials. Thus, combating corruption in customs bureaux should be a priority of SEE countries against transborder organized crime.

Corruption is a widespread phenomenon and not only related to the SEE. In 1996, economists of the International Monetary Fund (IMF) suggested that two per cent of the global gross domestic product was related to drug crime, and the sums of money associated with corruption and tax evasion would be an even larger percentage (Tanzi 1996). In fact, governments will never be able to totally eradicate corruption, as Klitgaard (1989) points out. At some point the marginal cost of reducing corruption will exceed the marginal benefits of doings so, and the economically optimal level of corruption will thus remain greater than zero. Yet extensive corruption, as in the SEE, jeopardizes the rule of law, as the observance, implementation and enforcement of the law becomes merely formal.[3] There is consensus among political scientists and economists that widespread corruption undermines democracy (Elliot 2002: 925) and a number of studies indicate that extensive corruption undermines development and proper functioning of the market (Gray and Kaufmann 1998; Ades and di Tella 1994; Mauro 1995; Wei 1997; Bardhan 1997).

Corruption in SEE countries is primarily attributed to the existence of weak state institutions.[4] Among these institutions, according to the Southeast European Legal Development Initiative (SELDI) survey (2002), the public perceives the customs department as one of the most corrupt institutions in SEE states (i.e. Albania, Bosnia and Herzegovina, Croatia, Macedonia, Romania and the Federal Republic of Yugoslavia) (USAID 2002; Velkova 2004: 40). In May 2002, the head of Kosovo's customs service was arrested on corruption charges (Transparency International 2003: 190). In 2002, the Bosnian Serb minister of finance resigned in a case of customs fraud that deprived the budget of US$15 million (ibid.: 197).

Indeed, customs departments in SEE are more vulnerable to corruption than other law enforcement agencies, because customs officers have direct discretionary access to tangible wealth, while being substantially underpaid. There are various international instruments which provide useful guidance for the SEE in fighting corruption in customs. The Arusha Declaration[5] provides the essential elements for effective anti-corruption strategy, the Kyoto Convention provides standards for modern custom procedures to facilitate international trade for greater economic growth,[6] and the OECD convention contains a set of guidelines in that respect.

On the other hand, comparative analyses of the anti-corruption customs reforms in central and eastern European states (CEE),[7] being directly related to the EU integration process to which the SEE countries also aspire, can provide the SEE countries with possible solutions to reduce corruption in customs organizations. The CEE countries have a similar past to that of the SEE countries, but unlike the latter, the CEE experienced custom reforms, and some of them showed progress in reducing corruption. Therefore, CEE legal reforms and experience can be helpful at least as a rule of thumb to help the SEE countries draft laws appropriate to their own circumstances and to find ways of enforcing them. On the basis of the CEE experience this article tries to identify possible measures that SEE countries could employ to fight corruption in customs departments, as an essential step in the battle against transborder organized crime.

First, the causes and current state of corruption in the customs administration in SEE countries are presented, followed by a brief overview of customs reforms in the CEE countries. It is argued that the SEE governments should establish strong and independent customs administrations by increasing accountability and transparency, and raising the salaries of custom officials.

CORRUPTION IN CUSTOMS AGENCIES IN SEE COUNTRIES

In general, customs agencies are prone to corruption as custom officers have direct discretionary access to tangible wealth. Customs agencies are normally responsible for implementing the foreign trade policy of the country and managing the customs rates, quantitative restrictions, rules of the origin of goods, anti-dumping measures and the like; preventing imports and general trafficking of undesirable and restricted goods, such as weapons, dangerous chemical substances, narcotics etc.; collecting considerable income from import and possible export taxes; and encouraging exports through customs rebates (holidays), tax holidays and other measures.

Related to the performance of these vital functions, various corrupt practices have been identified in the customs agencies of SEE counties, including routine corruption, occurring when private operators (consignee or consignor) pay bribes to smoothen custom procedures or accelerate them); fraudulent corruption, when private operators try to pay less tax than due, or no tax at all, by paying bribes to buy the custom officer's 'blind eye' or his active cooperation in avoiding proper customs clearance procedure; and criminal corruption, occurring when operators pay bribes to permit a completely illegal, lucrative operation (trafficking in drugs, weapons, people or abuse of export of promotion scheme etc.).

The officials often do not come directly into contact with the users of the customs services, but rather with their intermediaries. The forwarding agency transports goods from the place of departure to the place of destination. The owner of the goods has an interest in seeing his goods cross the border quickly, and therefore he allows the forwarding agency to bribe the customs officials, or they do it together. Often customs agents in SEE countries do not use their discretionary right to check the validity of transit documents and open sealed vehicles. The geographic position of SEE favours smuggling and various illegal activities, such as trafficking people. Quite often, goods enter the transit country but never leave. Corrupt customs officials might record that the freight actually left the country even if did not (Begovic et al. 2002: 118–20).

Why are customs officials in SEE among the most susceptible to such corrupt practices, and what explains the widespread corruption in the customs agencies of SEE? Various reasons are responsible for the corrupt behaviour of custom officials in SEE: low salaries and the impoverishment of state employees due to the collapse of the state sector, the introduction of economic sanctions on the Federal Republic of Yugoslavia and its economic isolation, ineffective penal policies, rigid trade policies and commercial protectionism in parallel with growth in the volume of trade, poor human resources management systems, and the almost unchecked power of customs officials.

Customs officials are susceptible to corrupt behaviour because they gain material or non-material benefits for themselves and their families. The transaction implies a two-way flow. A corrupt customs official violates customs clearance regulations and applies a lower tariff rate than required by law. The corrupter corrupts the custom official with money or other favours. According to Becker's model of the correlation of supply and demand and price the amount of the rent will depend on the demand for that corruption (service). The higher the amount of money that should be paid, the lower will be the amount demanded, and vice versa. Both parties have an interest in engaging in the corrupt behaviour, appropriation of rent and the elimination of the competitors.[8]

The latter is reinforced by the fact that customs officials in SEE are paid little beyond their subsistence minimum, which makes it difficult for them to rely exclusively on their regular income.[9] Customs officials' salaries are among the lowest in the field of public administration, yet there is great demand for getting jobs in the customs administration.

Moreover, the penal policy on corruption and its weak implementation creates a fertile environment for corruption in SEE. Becker's economic model of crime helps us understand the deterrence effect (the function of discouragement) of the punishment to the potential offender. If the ratio is positive, a potential offender will become an criminal; that is, he will commit the offence (Becker 1968).[10] With regard to customs officials, corruption may occur if the ratio is positive. Corruption in customs officials will depend on the value of the money (deal) or returned favour offered by corrupters and from the strictness of the penal policy and its implementation.[11] The greater the demand, the higher the value of the money or favour will be. The stricter the punishment and its enforcement, the less likely customs will be corrupt. A strict penal policy will decrease small-scale corruption, in which small amounts of money are involved, but will not necessarily reduce large-scale corruption.

The effectiveness of the penal policy depends on whether or not laws are implemented. In SEE, however, the judiciary is too weak to efficiently implement the penal policy with regard to corruption in customs agencies, because judges are not essentially independent. But even when judges are not corrupt, there is evidence that quite often judges in regular courts (or even specialized courts, e.g. commercial trade courts) are not familiar with the specific customs regulations and procedures. Customs regulations and procedures are based on international conventions, not domestic rules. There are cases that the courts might sometimes overturn, in the second ruling, a completely valid disciplinary measure of the customs administration due to lack of knowledge of the specific customs procedures (Begovic et al. 2002: 23).

Trade policies of protectionism in SEE, such as high customs tariff rates and non-tariff barriers for imports (contingents, licenses and quotas), create further incentives for illegal trade and therefore greater demand for corruption of customs officials.[12] Complicated customs procedures and the large number of different tariff rates applied to similar products also promote corruption. Under these circumstances, customs officials are tempted to misclassify the goods under a different tariff number where the customs duty is much lower.

Growth in the volume of trade and the resulting increase in the demand for services of customs administrations which, however, remain understaffed, has also lead to corruption. The long wait for regular service results in bribing customs officials in order to get service more quickly. These bribes resemble efficiency enhancing bribes if they are not linked with illegal activities.

A number of additional factors in customs corruption in SEE reflect the presence of organized crime. The Yugoslav embargo and the transition from a centralized economy to a market economy has created various illegal activities, such as smuggling and other kinds of organized criminal activities (trafficking of weapons, narcotics, aliens, cigarettes, coffee and alcohol). Corruption accompanied commerce in a wide range of primarily strategic commodities (petrol) and goods for mass consumption, such as coffee, cigarettes, toiletries and textiles. This corruption satisfied not only the interests of the individuals to make enormous profits but also of a large segment of the population to satisfy their basic needs.

Finally, the policy of human resource management in SEE plays an important role as a factor generating more corruption in customs organizations. Political leaders in SEE countries have strong influence on the selection, employment, promotion and dismissal of customs personnel (Begovic et al. 2002: 45). Many customs officials come from the border regions or surrounding areas where family ties and relations are very strong. The custom officer position is usually inherited from family members.

Discretionary interference of custom officials carried over from the socialist system – characterized by red tape, proliferation of regulations, and bureaucratic import–export quotas – creates a favourable transitional environment for corruption. The abuse of the existing foreign-trade system, import–export licenses and customs regulations reveals the existence of a bond between civil servants on different levels and in different spheres and crime. Ministries of finance and foreign trade issue import licenses, but customs agencies have the following discretionary rights: to verify the licenses issued or let the consignment pass without a license; to search any passenger and arrest him in cooperation with police, or confiscate property if the person who posses it infringes the customs regulation; to impose a duty on imported goods; and to asses the value of the consignment and determine its market value.

THE EXPERIENCE OF CEE CANDIDATE COUNTRIES IN CUSTOMS REFORMS

Corruption in the candidate countries has been one of the EU's concerns since its 1997 'Agenda 2000' report on CEE countries' applications for membership, because corruption undermines observation and implementation of EU law. In its regular report issued in October 2000, the commission found that corruption was systematic in Romania, a serious concern in Bulgaria, the Czech Republic, Poland and Slovakia and a continuing problem in Hungary, Latvia and Lithuania. The commission refrained from a critical assessment only in Slovenia and Estonia (European Commission 2000).

The secret services under the Communist regimes institutionalized smuggling in CEE states. The rise in the demand of imported goods after 1989 resulted in more customs vulnerability to corruption compared to other sectors of public administration.

What measures aimed at eradicating corruption in customs agencies have been adopted by the CEE candidate states during their preparation for the EU accession process, and how successful have these been?

The Czech Republic harmonized customs legislation with EU directives, and in 2001 was the first candidate state to be a signatory of the EU agreement on adopting a common transit regime and a new computerized transit system to simplify customs procedures and thus reduce corruption (Open Society Institute 2002: 181). In the Czech Republic, the same law regulates employment conditions for police and customs. The Customs Inspectorate is subordinate to the director general of the Customs Service.

Unlike the Ministry of Interior, the Inspectorate does not have the status of an agency of criminal investigation and can only notify the police to initiate criminal proceedings.

In December 1998, the Inspectorate approved the Integrity Action Plan divided into 12 areas: minimization of customs regulations, transparency, automation of customs procedures, personnel policy (including rotation of staff), management responsibility, control mechanism, morality and organizational culture, recruitment procedures to minimize the likelihood of recruiting corruptible staff, a code of ethical behaviour, expert training, increased pay and communication with exporters and importers. The major obstacle in the anti-corruption efforts was to rotate the staff due to a very high geographical immobility (ibid.: 181–2).

The Customs Board in Estonia introduced several measures. It established an Internal Control Department to conduct financial audits and monitor compliance with the Anti-Corruption Act and an Investigation Division and five investigation units to participate in the investigation of corruption cases. The government amended the procedural laws making corruption in customs agencies more difficult by introducing the compulsory presence of two officers ('four-eyes control'), division of tasks, rotation of staff and a six month probation period for new officers (ibid.: 228; European Commission 2000: 35).

Hungary set up a Central Investigation Office in 2000, with a staff of 130, as a Customs and Finance Guard, empowered to carry out investigations and introduce a reorganized and decentralization risk analysis system.[13]

Latvia introduced the following customs measures: a system of electronic declaration of goods,[14] a more precise delineation of duties and authorities of customs officers, a cooperation scheme with the Border Guard and staff rotation. Company surveys showed improvement between 1999 and 2001in the consistency of treatment by customs authorities (Latvian Development Agency 2001).

The Customs Department in Lithuania undertook the following reforms: provision of special equipment for customs offices and terminals, allowing more effective control of customs offices' work along with more operative inspection of customs activities, establishment of an Intelligence and Analysis Unit in 2000, approval of the Code of Ethics of Customs Officers (containing explicit instructions to avoid conduct regarded as a request for bribes) and signing a cooperation agreement with SIS to fight customs crime. In July 2001, the department and the established Division for Investigations in Office started to investigate the illegal activities of customs officials (Open Society Institute 2002: 386).

According to a Transparency International focus survey in March 2002, the customs administration in Slovakia is considered one of the most corrupt institutions, but there is no detailed research in this area. The newly established strategy for customs services outlines the importance of corruption prevention.

Slovenia made substantial progress in reducing the level of corruption in 1999–2000. Since it has experienced only one to two cases a year of disciplinary proceedings among 2,300 customs officials, the European Commission no longer mentions corruption as a problem in the customs administration of this country.

Slovenia undertook the following reforms: introduction of internal control units at each of the nine regional directorates (employing around 50–60 officers in total, and a special unit at the General Customs Directorate – 120 staff members). Under Slovenian law, corruption is a disciplinary offence. If there are grounds for suspicion of such an offence disciplinary procedures have to be initiated. Disciplinary procedures are independent of criminal procedures. Nonetheless, corruption is seen as a serious violation of employment responsibilities, leading to mandatory termination of the employee. Citizens may file complaints against the customs administration through a telephone hotline. The Customs Directorate introduced the Code of Conduct of Customs Officials in 2000. According to the code, customs officials should not accept bribes; in case they are found to have been bribed a three-member Ethical Arbitration Panel in the General Customs Directorate decides penalties (ibid.: 613–14).

World Bank reports in 1999 considered customs corruption in Poland as a serious problem (World Bank 1999: 19–20). According to the World Bank Diagnostic Survey of 2000, 66 per cent of companies believed that all or almost all customs officials are corrupt in Poland. Poland's EU accession process and the adoption of new procedures of customs inspections improved border-crossing procedures and reduced delays, important factors which had led to corruption. In 1997 Poland established the Customs Inspection Department with powers similar to the police. They introduced the rotation of staff officers every three years and the requirement for all customs officials to submit financial statements annually and upon taking and leaving office. They applied the 'many eyes' principle, i.e. the requirement for the presence of more than one officer at border inspections. In 2001, the president of the Customs Administration approved the Customs Ethics Code as a part of the anti-corruption strategy, providing an opportunity for citizens to submit information on malpractice via the Internet (Open Society Institute 2002: 440–42).

Romania and Bulgaria provide interesting cases because these belong to the SEE region. Customs corruption in Romania is due to the country's position as an important transit route for trafficking various illegal goods. For example, according to one investigative journalist, the price to secure the post of head of the Customs Authority was €1.3m (interview with Nicoleta Savin, journalist at *Evenimentul Zilei*, 29 March 2002). Corruption practices in customs agencies were seriously checked by the Romanian Intelligence Unit during the Yugoslav embargo. According to the GRECO evaluation report, Romania introduced asset monitoring for customs officials in 1995, and, in January 2001, compulsory tax returns to monitor the discrepancies between lifestyle and declared assets. However, the country lacked the ability to introduce special training to prevent corruption of customs staff (GRECO 2002: 21).

In Bulgaria, between October 1997 and 1999, the Customs Department fired 102 officers because of proven offences against customs legislation (Centre for the Study of Democracy 2000: 17). In 1998 86 per cent of foreign cigarettes imported to Bulgaria were imported illegally. This figure reached 90 per cent in 2001 (ibid.: 43). In the early 2000s the government introduced reforms in the customs administration as a part of its general anti-corruption strategy. The new appointed director of Customs Administration established an Internal Control Department within the Customs Agency and announced new investigative powers for customs officers. He dismissed the head of the regional customs agency (in Rousse), and replaced other customs officials there, because that unit collected bribes for a high-ranking official in the Customs Agency in Sofia (Open Society Institute 2002: 123). The Customs Agency in Sofia opened a 24-hour hotline to facilitate reports on corruption. However, after announcing a contract with a foreign company for advice on customs reforms, which provoked a strong reaction, the director was forced to resign.

CONCLUSION

The geographic position of SEE and CEE countries as transit countries favours organized crime, both transnational and national. SEE countries share similarities with the CEE: the establishment and consolidation of newly formed customs authorities, strong political influence in customs employment policy, transitional economies, low salaries for state employees, and lack of transparency and accountability.

The CEE experience in fighting corruption in customs agencies might provide possible solutions for the reform of customs agencies in SEE countries. Clearly the substantial customs reforms in the CEE countries have led to a decline in corruption levels in customs agencies. Of course, one-size-fits-all solutions do not work. The experience of the CEE countries cannot be simply copied in the SEE. Cultural, historical and other differences are great and are reflected in differences in the extent and nature of corruption in customs agencies. For example, customs corruption in the Czech Republic is likely to be influenced not only by the Communist legacy but also the historical legacy of the Habsburg Empire and the bureaucratic tradition it left. In Poland, customs corruption more likely results from the centuries-old distrust borne of their history of occupation by various external powers. Nor do all these countries have equal resources. All these differences suggest that there is a need for a specific solution for each country.

Nonetheless, some reform measures adopted by the CEE countries might be useful to SEE governments which seek to fight customs corruption. These reform measures include reducing the number of customs regulations; introducing transparency and automation in customs procedures; introducing a 24-hour hotline to facilitate corruption reports; introducing electronic declaration of goods; issuing customs officers a code of ethics, explaining the penalties and the behaviour expected; introducing an Ethical Arbitration Panel to decide penalties; establishing internal control units within the regional directorates; amending the procedural law to include compulsory presence of two officers ('four-eyes control'), a division of tasks, the characterization of corruption as a disciplinary offence and a serious violation of employment ethics leading to mandatory termination; establishing a Customs Department to investigate the illegal activities of customs officials; applying sound human resource management policies relating to adequate remuneration, promotion, objective staff reporting, rotation of staff, and a six-month probation period for new officers; training experts to prevent and combat customs staff corruption; and increasing the salaries of customs officials; improving communication with exporters and importers.

One thing is certain: SEE countries must establish strong and independent customs administrations by increasing accountability, transparency, and payment of customs officials and by implementing the Kyoto Convention measures for trade facilitation. The anti-corruption and trade facilitation measures will combat transborder organized crime and foster international trade, which, in turn, will result in greater economic growth for SEE countries on their way to integration into the EU. Of course, more general reforms should aim at eradicating widespread corruption in other important segments of the state institutional structure, including the judiciary and the remaining law-enforcement agencies in SEE states.

NOTES

1. The US Criminal Profiteering Act, 1985 defines organized crime as the act of organizing, directing or financing a least three persons with the intent to engage in a pattern of criminal profiteering activity, or inciting third parties to engage in violence or intimidation with the same intent. See also Joint Action of 29 November adopted by the European Council on the basis of Article K.3 of the EU Treaty, concerning the creation and maintenance of a directory of specialized competencies, skills and expertise in the fight against international organized crime, in order to facilitate law enforcement cooperation between Member States of the EU, OJL 342/2, 1996.

2. Romania presents a lot of evidence for dealing with drug distribution routes to Europe through Hungary. There are suspicions that Romanians also produce the drugs. The Romanian Information Service estimates that 60 per cent of the drugs entering Romania from all sources transit through Turkey. See ⟨http://www.ogd.org/rapport/gb/RP07_4_ROUMANIE.html⟩. There are reports that Bulgarians are involved in the drug trade, gambling and prostitution, and in selling weapons and narcotics. Bulgarians have also taken part in smuggling nuclear materials and explosives. See ⟨http://www.ogd.org/gb/29EBUUGAA.html⟩, ⟨http://www.ogd.org/gb/21EBUWFA.html⟩ and ⟨http://www.alternatives.com/crime/ENV2.HTML⟩. Coming from a total isolation and a totalitarian regime, Albanian contraband profited from the regional crises and oil and arms embargos. Albanians also collaborate with Italian and Greek criminals for the smuggling of humans, hashish and marijuana. Ethnic Albanians from Macedonia and Kosovo hold a share of drug markets of Austria, Germany, Hungary, the Czech Republic, Poland and Belgium, and almost exclusively supply the Swiss market (Muco 1999).

3. According to the World Bank (2000), there are two types of corruption in transition countries: state capture (illicit provision of gains to public officials to influence the formation of the laws, regulations, decrees and other government policies) and administrative corruption (the illicit provisions of gains to public officials to distort the implementation of existing rules, laws and regulations).

4. The economic analyses indicate a positive correlation between weak state institutions and corruption (Abed and Davoodi 2000).

5. The key factors of the revised Arusha Declaration are leadership and commitment at the management level, a simplified regulatory framework, transparency to enhance predictability, an appeal mechanism, automation to reduce opportunities for corruption, reform and modernization for faster and more friendly customs (to eliminate the temptation to bribe officers), audit and investigation capabilities, a code of conduct, human resource management (selection, training, salary, promotion, rotation, training and performance appraisal), morale and organizational culture (pride in customs agency) and a relationship with private investors.

6. The Kyoto Convention entered into force in 1974 with the objective to simplify and harmonize customs procedures. The World Custom Organization (WCO) revised and updated its objectives in 1999 to ensure that they meet the current demands of international trade. The key elements of the revised Kyoto Convention for Customs Reforms to Promote Trade Facilitation are the maximum use of automated systems, the use of electronic funds transfer, risk management techniques, coordination with other agencies, easy access to the information on customs procedures, laws, rules and regulations by any person, a transparent system of complaints in the customs procedure and a creation of consultative relations with the trade. See ⟨http://www.wcoomd.org/ie/En/Past_Events/trade99/kyotoe.html⟩. Although the WCO can oversee and enforce the Kyoto Convention it lacks a 'dispute settlement' mechanism to enforce the required procedures.

7. The central and eastern European states are Bulgaria, the Czech Republic, Estonia, Hungary, Latvia, Lithuania, Poland, Romania, Slovakia and Slovenia.

8. In the first case, despite the normal profit the corrupter appropriates rent equal to the unpaid customs duty, reduced by the amount of the bribe paid. In the second case, the main motivation of the corrupter is to eliminate competitors in his industry and lead

them to bankruptcy or liquidation or even to leave the industry. By eliminating his competitors, the corrupter gains economic profit by having a monopoly in the particular industry.

9. Corruption has a social explanation in low wages. Economic analyses indicate a positive correlation between crime and low wages (see Van Rijckeghem and Weder 1997; Tanzi 1998).

10. Becker's basic contention is that all individuals are rational utility maximizers, and when they decide whether to commit a particular crime or not they compare the utility they would gain by using their type and other resources in the pursuit of legal endeavours. According to Becker, an individual becomes a criminal not so much because his motivation differs from that of other individuals, but because his conception of the costs and benefits of criminal acts is different or perhaps his attitude to risk is different (Pyle 1984: 10).

11. Among the factors that influence an individual's decision to engage in corrupt behaviour are the expected gains from crime relative to earnings from legal work, the risk of being caught and convicted, the extent of punishment, and the opportunities in legal activities (see Witte and Witt 2001). The levels of crime will depend on the actual effect of deterrence, the will of the enforcement agencies to implement the public will, and social factors (such as family disorder) (Glaser 1999).

12. Economic cross-country data analyses indicate a positive correlation between the effect of corruption on wealth and the degree of a country's openness (see Neeman, Paserman and Simhon 2003).

13. According to Gallup's research in 2000, 28 per cent of surveyed people considered customs officials and borders guards as corrupt, and 37 per cent of SMEs surveyed expected to face corruption when seeking clearance of goods. See ⟨http://www.gallup.hu/Gallup/monitor/en/gsurveys/010119_pubinst.html⟩ and ⟨http://www.gallup.hu/Gallup/monitor/en/gsurveys/010129_business.html⟩.

14. The Revised Kyoto Convention helps governments cope with the challenges of electronic trade for fast and efficient goods clearance. The term '"electronic trade' refers to a method of performing the current trade and it is a technique for exchange of trade information. The convention requires the customs agency to apply technologies to reduce the cost in customs activities and trade.

REFERENCES

Abed, George T. and Hamid R. Davoodi (2000): *Corruption, Structural Reforms, and Economic Performance in the Transition Economies*, IMF Working Paper, WP/00/132. Washington, DC: International Monetary Fund.

Ades, Alberto and Rafael di Tella (1994): *Competition and Corruption*, Working Paper, Oxford: University Institute of Economics and Statistics.

Bardhan, Pranab (1997): 'Corruption and Development: A Review of Issues', *Journal of Economic Literature*, 35, pp.1320–46.

Becker, Gary (1968): 'Crime and Punishment: An Economic Approach', *Journal of Political Economy*, 76, pp.169–217.

Begovic, B., M. Vasovic, S. Vukovic, B. Mijatovic R. Sepi (2002): *Korupcija na carini*. Belgrade.

Elliot, K.A. (2002): 'Corruption as an International Policy Problem', in A.J. Heidenheimer and M. Johnson, eds, *Political Corruption: Concepts & Contexts*, 3rd ed (New Brunswick, NJ: Transaction Publishers).

European Commision (2000): *Corruption Report Summary*, ⟨http://www.eumap.org/whatsnew/pressinfo/1038254774/index_html?print=1⟩.

Glaser, Edward L. (1999): Harvard University and NBER, Preliminary Draft, 1999.

Gray, C.W. and D. Kaufmann (1998): 'Corruption and Development', *Finance and Development*, March, pp.7–11.

GRECO (2002): *Evaluation Report on Romania*. Strasbourg: Groupe d'Etats contra la corruption.
Klitgaard, Robert (1989): *Controlling Corruption*. Berkeley, CA: University of California Press.
Latvian Development Agency (2001): *2001 Survey on the Business Environment in Latvia*, ⟨www.lda.gov.lv/images/2001anal_for_internet.doc⟩.
Mauro, Paolo (1995): 'Corruption and Growth', *Quarterly Journal of Economics*, 110:2, pp.681–712.
Muco, Marta (1999): 'Corruption and Public Governance in Southeastern European Transition Countries: The case of Albania' paper presented at the Joint LSE-WIIW Conference on Reconstruction and Integration in Southeast Europe: Economic Aspects, Vienna, 12–13 November 1999.
Neeman, Zivka, M. Daniele Paserman and Avi Simhon (2003): 'Corruption and Openness', unpublished paper..
Open Society Institute (2002): *Monitoring the EU Accession Process*. Budapest: Open Society Institute.
Pyle, David J. (1984): *The Economics of Crime and Law Enforcement*. London: MacMillan.
Tanzi, Vito (1996): *Money Laundering and the International Financial Systems*, IMF Working Paper No.96, 55. Washington, DC: International Monetary Fund.
Tanzi, Vito (1998): 'Corruption Around the World, Causes, Consequences, Scope and Cures', *IMF Staff Papers*, 45:4, pp.572–4.
Transparency International (2003): *Global Corruption Report*. Berlin: Transparency International.
USAID (2002): *Regional Corruption Monitoring in Albania, Bosnia and Herzegovina, Bulgaria, Croatia, Macedonia, Romania and Yugoslavia*. Sofia: Vitosha Research.
Van Rijckeghem, Caroline and Beatrice Weder (1997): *Corruption and the Rate of Temptation: Do Low Wages in Civil Service Cause Corruption?*, IMF Working Paper WP/97/93. Washington, DC: International Monetary Fund.
Velkova, Emi (2004): 'European Anti-Corruption Initiatives in SEE', *Denver Journal of International Law and Policy*, forthcoming 2004.
Viano, Emilio C. (1999): Global Organized Crime and International Security, 1999, p. 13-21.
Wei, Shang-Jin (1997): *How Taxing is Corruption on International Investors?* Cambridge, MA: Kennedy School of Government.
Witte, Ann Dryden and Robert Witt (2001): 'Crime Causation: Economic Theories', in *Encyclopedia of Crime and Justice* (London: MacMillan).
World Bank (1999): *Corruption in Poland*. Warsaw: World Bank.
World Bank (2000): *Anti-Corruption in Transition: A Contribution to the Policy Debate*. Washington, DC: World Bank.

Transborder Crime between Turkey and Greece: Human Smuggling and its Regional Consequences

AHMET İÇDUYGU

INTRODUCTION

Saying that national boundaries are often a source of both *conflict* and *cooperation* between neighbours is an understatement. By their very nature, borders and border crossings emerge as areas of unresolved issues of governance within and between nation-states (Jordan and Düvell 2003). The flows of goods, capital, and people crossing borders pose problems for the neighbouring countries, and consequently for relations between them. When border crossings happen in an irregular manner, then they pose even more problems. Today, irregular border crossings are multiplying everywhere (Berdal and Serano 2002). The Turkish–Greek border – a land border of more than 203 kilometres and the lengthy and curvy coast of the Aegean Sea – is no exception to such crossings.

Due to a long history of tension and conflict, Greece and Turkey attract considerable attention in the international relations literature (see Kollias and Günlük-Şenesen 2003), but transborder crimes do not usually feature in academic writings on these two countries. This article looks at the main challenges transborder crimes between these two countries give rise to and assesses the responses of these countries to these challenges. It specifically focuses on the smuggling of migrants from Turkey to Greece. In the conclusion, it also addresses the wider context of these challenges within the context of the security and irregular migration regimes in Europe.

There is no doubt that transborder crimes between Turkey and Greece are not solely limited to human smuggling. Illegal cross-border transactions of all kinds exist. The Turkey–Greece border line straddles several main transportation routes linking Asia and Africa with western Europe; as a consequence, it has become a significant transit area for smuggling and trafficking of different kinds (mainly drug trafficking and human smuggling, but probably even arm trafficking) operating along those routes. National and international authorities believe that only a small portion of the illegal goods and migrants that enter these countries end up on the local market; the vast bulk of the traffic passes through bound for western Europe. This article focuses solely on tackling smuggling in human beings. Given the growing importance of tragic cases of human smuggling, and their devastating effects on the social and political institutions of the European countries, it is not surprising that these problems have recently come to the forefront in many European countries, including Turkey and Greece.

Border-crossing pathways, whether regular or irregular, are not random; they usually follow economic connections and historical links (Jordan and Düvell 2003: 62). Situated in the eastern Mediterranean basin, the Turkish–Greek land borders and coastlines not only serve as a gateway to the Balkan region, but also operate as a transit zone at the east–west and north–south crossroads. In other words, this region is part of the European frontier, representing 'a sharp, even brutal divide between "developed" Europe and the much less-developed realms of North Africa and the Middle East' (King 1998: 109). Therefore, it is not surprising that the direction of the transfrontier flows of goods, capital and people in this region is from east to west and from south to north: thus, as far as the flows between Turkey and Greece are concerned, the main direction is from the former to the latter. It is within this context that border crossings constitute a concern for both countries, but it is not symmetrical. Both countries share a desire to control movements of goods, capital and people. However, unsuccessful management of these movements in either country is likely to be felt more by Greece since it is far more likely to be the target, given its pulling position in Europe as being a part of the continent. In other words, Greece's position in Europe is far more attractive than Turkey's position; consequently, Greece has a considerably greater economic stake in regulating the movements of goods and people between countries.

DOCUMENTING THE UNDOCUMENTED: HUMAN SMUGGLING BETWEEN GREECE AND TURKEY

In September 2003, various news agencies reported that the decaying bodies of at least 24 illegal immigrants were found by a military patrol on the banks of the border river between Turkey and Greece and officials said the immigrants, believed to be from Pakistan, probably had drowned four or five days earlier (see, for instance, Agence France Press, 10 September 2003). They were attempting to cross from Turkey into Greece, with the help of smugglers, across the river which flows into the Aegean Sea when their overladen boat capsized. According to the authorities, this was the worst accident involving illegal immigrants for more than three years. Three months later, in December 2003, news agencies reported the worst accident ever of its kind in the area between Turkey and Greece (see, for instance, *Sabah* newspaper, 25 December 2003). An estimated 60 people were drowned in the Mediterranean after a boat carrying illegal migrants sank in mild weather within sight of the Greek island of Rhodes. The vessel was carrying Iraqi, Afghan and Jordanian migrants, a Turkish coast-guard official said. A passing ferry picked up one survivor, an Iraqi, while search and rescue teams from Turkey and Greece found only the boat's tiller and an empty life jacket. The only survivor told the police that the smugglers left them alone and escaped when the boat was sinking. These incidents indicated once more that the flow of illegal migrants from Turkey to Greece still continues.

Before going into the details of the main discussion here, a conceptual clarification is certainly necessary. Drawing upon the nature of border crossing between Turkey and Greece, what is discussed in this article is human smuggling rather than human trafficking. Trafficking differs from smuggling in two points (İçduygu and Toktaş 2002). First, exploitation is a fundamental element of the various phases of trafficking whereas the foremost characteristic of smuggling is not exploitation. Second, although smuggling suggests an illegal entry of a person into a foreign country encompassing an international migration aspect, human trafficking may not necessarily involve any border crossing.

According to the police reports and media coverage of human smuggling incidents, there are two main types of route used for smuggling of irregular migrants from Turkey to Greece. The first is on foot, crossing the land border via the Evros River, also known as the Meric. The second is by boat, sailing from Turkey to the eastern Aegean islands or to the Greek mainland. Partly due to their nature and partly because of lack of sound data, various aspects of migrant smuggling between Turkey and Greece are still relatively unknown; what we know is often merely a bit more than speculation. As the main concern here is to go beyond speculation and description, this article makes use of numerous sources of information to investigate the two main routes of smuggling, namely land border and coastline crossings. The data used for the elaboration of the land border crossings are borrowed from (a) empirical migration research conducted in Edirne, the Turkish province bordering Greece, in 2002 (Yılmaz 2003), and (b) a secondary analysis of available data from the Turkish Ministry of Interior (BFBA 2001a,b). The information on sea crossings is derived from the International Maritime Organization (IMO).[1] The analysis of the data and the discussion here covers the seven-year period from 1997 to 2003. This period was interesting and significant because, within this period, migration flows increased, reached a peak and started to decline. Furthermore, Greece, Turkey and other European countries started to pay more attention to the issue. As will be discussed in detail in the following parts of the article, the readmission agreement signed between Turkey and Greece in November 2001 was a result of the greater importance attached to the irregular migration flows between the two countries.

It is of course impossible to provide an accurate figure for the proportion of irregular, or smuggled, migrants who have travelled on foot or by sea. However, it is possible to give some estimated figures. Information obtained from the Turkish Ministry of Interior gives an indication of the number of irregular migrants apprehended in Turkey over the seven years between 1997 and 2003 and signals very clear trends. Only 11,000 irregular migrants were apprehended in the country in 1997. From some 29,000 irregular migrants apprehended in 1998, the figure rose to over 47,000 by 1999. The figure nearly doubled to 94,000 in 2000, reaching its peak over the period. Numbers declined to 92,000 in 2001, some 84,000 in 2002 and below 50,000 in 2003. The total number of irregular migrants apprehended in the whole period was over 400,000 (İçduygu 2003b). In the same period, nearly 70,000 irregular migrants were apprehended in Edirne province of Turkey near the Greek border while they were trying to depart for Greece (calculated from figures in Yılmaz 2003). This figure indicates that almost one-sixth of the irregular migrants in Turkey were those who were attempting to go to Greece. Among them the majority were Iraqis (31 per cent), Iranians (20 per cent) and Pakistanis (10 per cent). Irregular migrants from Afghanistan, Bangladesh, Palestine,

India and Turkey together accounted for 33 per cent of the total number of the apprehended people who were about to depart for Greece.

The 2002 Edirne study of irregular migrants indicated that a quarter of these migrants entered Turkey with the help of smugglers. Almost all of them hoped to be helped by smugglers to leave the country. The major target countries for final destinations were the United Kingdom (14 per cent), Germany (13 per cent), Greece (13 per cent), Italy (6 per cent) and France (5 per cent). On average, the total cost per person to migrate through Turkey was US$1,660; a large portion of this amount was given to smugglers. Almost one in every ten had previously attempted to leave Turkey with the assistance of smugglers, but had been unsuccessful in their efforts. Three per cent of the interviewed migrants said that they previously managed to go to Greece from Turkey but were apprehended there and deported back to Turkey. Only a quarter of the irregular migrants indicated they would consider going back to their homeland as an alternative; the others stated that they would try to sneak into Europe via Greece at any cost and were willing to pay the smugglers to facilitate their trips. The migrants interviewed reported further that they were expecting to be guided into Greece by the smugglers either by crossing the Evros River (by boat or swimming, and where and if the water was shallow, on foot) or by walking over the land border in Karaağaç region of Edirne province.

In addition to travelling on foot, use of sea vessels became increasingly common in human smuggling from Turkey to Greece over the second half of the 1990s. According to the biannual IMO Reports, between 1998 and 2002 the total number of reported coastal incidents associated with the trafficking or transport of illegal migrants in the Mediterranean basin was 431, involving 16,425 irregular migrants. Among these reported cases, 275 were Turkish–Greek cases in which 7,325 irregular migrants were trying to enter Greece from Turkey illegally. These figures indicate that within this five-year period almost two-thirds of the incidents associated with trafficking or transporting of illegal migrants in the Mediterranean Basin were between Turkey and Greece, involving more than 45 per cent of apprehended irregular migrants.

Various types of sea vessels were used to smuggle irregular migrants from Turkey to Greece, including inflated, two-meter-long rowboats boarding 17 persons, a 12-meter-long, plastic luxury yacht with cabins carrying 58 persons, and a 28-meter-long wooden boat with 188 passengers. The vast majority of these voyages started from various parts of the Turkish Aegean coastline such as Çanakkale, İzmir and Muğa. The objective was to reach the nearest islands of the eastern Aegean such as Samos, Kos or Rhodes, while some of them were heading to the Greek mainland. There were very sharp changes in the numbers of these boat people over time: from 16 in 1999 and 18 in 2000, the figure had risen to 119 in 2001; it dropped to 102 in 2002, and to less than 50 in 2003.

SMUGGLING, OR *KAÇAKÇILIK*, FROM TURKEY TO GREECE: MECHANISMS AND NEW TRENDS

The smuggling business in Turkey is organized by the *kaçakçılar* (plural). A *kaçakçı* (singular) is a person who facilitates the illegal entry of a person into a foreign country. It has been widely argued that smuggling, or *kaçakçılık*, of migrants. especially to the European continent, is a monopoly of organized groups that dedicate themselves to these activities exclusively (Di Nicola 1999). Smugglers are assumed to get involved in human smuggling as a result of experience acquired in other kinds of illegal activities. In other words, as international entrepreneurs who monitor the opportunities and risks connected with various types of crime in the countries in which they operate, smugglers shift from one illicit activity to another, spreading their operative sectors on the basis of mere opportunistic criteria (ibid.: 4). The common view is that smuggling and other organized crimes are closely interrelated (Salt 2000). However, here I will argue that the human smuggling business does not always involve large networks of smugglers organized through mafia-like structure, at least in Turkey. It seems that smaller organizations, if any, employ diverse and flexible mechanisms of human smuggling. My recent research shows that as far as the smugglers in Turkey and their associates abroad are concerned, there is no or very little top-down centralized hierarchy among these people of different nationalities and origins (İçduygu 2003a). In other words, contrary to the majority of literature reviews on international illegal migration, the process is not organized fully at an international level. Smuggling of migrants in Turkey, unlike the smuggling or trafficking of drugs or arms, does not usually operate through a centralized international network.

If there is no central organization in the smuggling of migrants, how is it that a traveller starting off from Kabul or Baghdad makes his way, by completely illegal means, to Istanbul, and then to Athens, or to London, or even across the continent to New York or Melbourne? The answer to this question lies in the concept of networks (Papadopoulou 2002). On the route from Afghanistan to Istanbul, or from Iraq to Athens, there is a large network consisting of hundreds people in smaller networks who are independent and yet connected to one another. The larger network maintains its survival due to the flexibility and creativity of the smaller networks of professional and amateur smugglers with different jobs and specializations. Thus, the fact that small breaks and leaks do occur within the larger network does not in fact threaten the survival of the whole. A new small piece that becomes a part of the whole, or an old piece that adapts itself to the new conditions, ensures the continuation of the system with no problems. Thus, we are confronted with the sum of smaller 'local' organizations, rather than international centralized organizations.

As I argue elsewhere, in general, illegal migrants are taken from city to city or from country to country via 'hand-to-hand' or 'smuggler-to-smuggler' approaches (İçduygu and Toktaş: 2002). The migrant, who illegally crosses the border, is handed over to another smuggler in the country of arrival and continues on his route. Because of the large number of smugglers on the route, the smugglers in the country of destination are unaware of the smugglers in the country of departure. For instance, a smuggler who lives in Ipsala, a Turkish border town in Edirne province, has, based on his network, a contact with a smuggler who lives in Alexandroupolis, a Greek city close to Turkish border. But it is less likely that the smuggler in Alexandroupolis will have contact with a smuggler in Van, a Turkish border city neighbouring Iran, which hosts many irregular migrants as an entry point to Turkey. It is even less likely that the smuggler in Alexandroupolis has any contact with a smuggler in Baghdad, Tehran or Kabul. Even if they have a contact, it is mostly a relative or a friend who assists through mobile phone connections, indicating larger network ties. Given the smaller networks mostly based on national and ethnic affiliations, smugglers are acquainted only with the smugglers they receive migrants from and those to whom they hand over migrants. They have no chances of meeting and relating to other smugglers who make up the remaining pieces of the larger chain. It is for this reason that the chain of smugglers may break. In addition to this, the pieces of the chain are extremely volatile. As the middlemen in Istanbul report, migrants are not handed over to a particular smuggler, but to one who, at that specific moment, owns the means of transportation and is prepared to handle the remaining part of the journey. Meanwhile, the existing division of labour among smugglers leads to the expansion of the network. For instance, the smaller network which prepares the necessary fake ID cards and passports for illegal migrants works for all the smugglers in a particular region, and sometimes even for illegal political organizations. There are specific networks that provide fake visas by changing the dates on expired Schengen visas. Therefore, it would be possible to include in the larger network of traffickers such independent groups as these dealing exclusively with the provision of fake documents such as passports, visas, ID cards and so on.

Other groups that help expand the network of illegal migration are the landlords who rent their houses as illegal migrant dormitories for the accommodation of hundreds of migrants in places like İstanbul, İzmir,

Çanakkale; the small hotel operators who are revealed after every police operation but continue to act as home-providers for passing illegal travellers; the bus, minibus, pick-up truck and truck owners and drivers who take the migrants to the airport, the dock where they are loaded onto ships, or villages close to the western borders. All these actors are pieces in the chain and help expand and deepen the network. These groups, like the groups which prepare fake documents, provide their services in exchange for money. For this reason, there is both competition and cooperation among these groups. They carry out their activities not as members of a large central organization for illegal migration, but as independent pieces which form only a small part of the network.

Within this extensive network, there is a natural mechanism of trustworthy intermediaries who are members of different national and ethnic groups. These are 'leaders' who have mostly travelled the same route themselves as illegal migrants, have legally or illegally resided in the countries on the route of illegal migration, and serve as guides to those who follow. Even if they are not personally involved, they act as natural guides to those who are directly involved in the business of illegal migration. While some of these people act directly as smugglers, taking migrants to the West, others act as cashiers by playing the role of the middlemen and establishing contact between the smuggler and migrants from their hometown.

Based on these connections, someone who leaves Afghanistan or Iraq knows beforehand whom to contact once he or she is in Tehran or Istanbul, or Edirne or Alexandroupolis, or Athens. These irregular migrants often have in their hands the names, addresses or telephone numbers of the middlemen or smugglers they would be contacting once they reach a certain destination. On the other hand, the smuggler or the middleman who receives information prior to the start of the migrants' journey knows about the number of migrants that will be arriving, the countries they wish to go and the fake documents they will need on the way. Therefore, he is able to make arrangements for accommodation and other needs before the migrants arrive.

Technological development and the knowledge created by globalization results in the creation of a network and the establishment of communication among the smugglers themselves as well as between smugglers and illegal migrants. This enables the pieces of the chain to form links with one another, despite the absence of a central structure. This is confirmed by a security officer who, talking about the smuggling in the border region of Van province in Turkey, tells of a shepherd who had in his pocket 2 GSM cards and a mobile phone. These recent developments have created an opportunity for smugglers to escape the control of the security forces and to meet easily with other smugglers in the dark, even up in the mountains, as opposed to the old techniques of meeting each other by marking stones near the borders. There is evidence that, for instance, a mobile phone enables a woman in the United States to contact and make a deal with a smuggler who holds her sister captive in the mountains between Iran and Turkey (İçduygu 2003a). There are also cases which show how illegal migrants from Iraq are able to contact middlemen on the Istanbul–Edirne–Alexandroupolis–Athens route. These examples indicate that the business of illegal migration keeps up with the times and takes full advantage of technological developments.

According to official figures in Turkey, 1,155 people were arrested for smuggling migrants in 2001. There were 1,157 smugglers apprehended in 2002. In the last three years there has been a tremendous increase in the number of smugglers. While the number of smugglers arrested in 1998 was 98, this number increased to 187 in 1999 and 850 in 2000. As far as 2002 is concerned, almost 90 per cent of the apprehended smugglers were Turkish citizens, while the majority of the remainder were Iraqis, Iranians, Greeks and Bangladeshis. If one adds the estimated number of illegal migrants who made their way into Europe through Turkey without getting caught by security forces to the total number of illegal migrants apprehended in Turkey in the early 2000s, one can estimate that the total number of illegal migrants who pass through Turkey is not less than 200,000 annually. Considering that each migrant spends an average of $1,500, the total amount of money involved in the business per year is $300 million. The amount of money involved in the human smuggling business reflects its economic importance. This requires a separate analysis at the level of the political economy of the whole business, something that is beyond the scope of this short article.

Although probably not comparable to the amounts of money involved in drug trafficking, profits from human smuggling are also very high.[2] The transfer of funds by the smugglers, in a complicated system from border to border and city to city, and based on ethnic affiliations and connections, is a complex matter. Among Iraqi nationals, the migrant hands the requested money to a third person who is known and trusted by the smuggler. When the migrant reaches the destination (such as Istanbul or Athens) he calls the cashier and, with the use of a previously selected password, assures that the money reaches the smuggler. The cashier gets a commission from the smuggler for this business. While Iraqi smugglers use the method of a trustworthy third party as cashier in their dealings with migrants, smugglers of other nationalities and ethnic groups use the 'cash in advance' method. A different method applies in the case of Afghan migrants. No cash is being used in these cases. Those who intend to migrate from Afghanistan agree to hand over their houses upon departure.

The smuggler who takes possession of the house then agrees to meet all the costs of the migrants during their trip to the country of destination. Iraqi and Afghan cases are exceptions within the larger picture. The main rule in the smuggling of migrants is 'cash in advance'. In fact, no money is found on illegal migrants and smugglers when they are caught in ships, trucks or other vehicles. This is an indication that money changes hands between the migrant and the smuggler prior to the start of the journey. As reported by the migrants themselves, even if they are caught on the way, the smuggler usually keeps his promise and the migrant is eventually taken to the point of destination.

It is also the case that some illegal migrants do not make the arrangements for their country of destination with the smugglers in their country of departure. Migrants generally cross borders with the help of local smugglers and the money is paid to each smuggler for the border crossing or the smaller portion of the route taken. For instance, a migrant who pays $150 for the journey from Iran to Turkey pays another smuggler $250–$300 for the trip from Van to Istanbul (the amount increases if fake documents are included). Extra money is again paid for the trip from Istanbul to Alexandroupolis, Athens or elsewhere. However, this method of payment has other risks. There are plenty of cases, for instance, in which migrants who carry money or belongings are robbed. In border crossings, if arrangements are made between smugglers, the smuggler who hands over the migrant to the next smuggler gives a share of the total money previously paid by the migrant to the initial smuggler. This procedure is repeated for other arrangements made along the way. The money, shrinking as it goes further, travels the same route as the migrants. As evidenced in face-to-face interviews with the smugglers (İçduygu 2003a), from the moment the bargain is made in the country of departure, the money is divided up among a number of smugglers on the route and finds its way to the country of arrival piecemeal. Here are some descriptions how the money travels (ibid: 92):

> I used to hire foreign workers in my textile workshop in Süleyman-iye [a district in Istanbul] because they were cheaper. In 1996, Afghani Amjet Sertil who was one of the workers working in my workshop told me that with his 5 other friends he would go to Europe. He told me that they had made the arrangements but wanted to entrust me with 9,000 dollars for six people. He wanted me to give the money to a person that he specified after they reached Europe. He introduced me to Muammer Küçük, the owner of Ülkü Nakliyat on Fatih Fevzipaşa street, and asked me to give the 9,000 dollars to Muammer Küçük after he called me up from Europe.

Amjet went to Europe. After some time, he phoned me and told me to hand the money over to Muammer Küçük. Muammer Küçük came to me and I gave him the 9,000 dollars. By this way, I learned that Muammer Küçük smuggled people abroad. The foreign workers of Afghani and Iraqi origin who were working for me at the workshop also wanted to go to Europe. I sent groups of 10, 15, 30 people to Muammer Küçük at different times. Muammer Küçük was giving me 150 dollars per person. In the meantime, the businesses at Laleli [district of unregistered export] have stopped. I closed my shop and started to do only this job.

Once the person or a relative of the person gets in touch with me, the money is paid to my relative in that country [Greece]. The money is then transferred to my account in the Taksim branch of Interbank. Sometimes when my partner goes abroad to collect the passports, he meets up with the intermediaries and personally collects and brings back the money.

In smuggling the money is paid in advance. The smuggler will buy or rent a ship, prepare the passports, bribe for the visas and pay for the hotel or the house. Why should he have to pay from his own pocket? For this reason, money is always collected beforehand. Even if the payment is made abroad, it is taken in advance and then the travellers are transported. It is because of this that no money is found on travellers who are caught on ships or in trucks. This is the basic rule in all smuggling business: money first!

It does not matter whether the coastman or I collect the money. If I collect the money, I take my share and give the rest to the other smuggler friends. If he collects it, he gives me my percentage. The money gets paid up front in this business. In case of an accident, the responsibility is ours. I mean, if the person gets caught, his money does not go to trash. For the next trial, we take him to the place he wants for free.

We gave the money here [Hungary] to a cook. 700 dollars for Slovakia, 120 dollars for Austria per person. He gave us the code in return. When my wife and I reach Austria, I will telephone the cook and tell him the code. He will give the money to the smuggler that we had made the deal with.

Human smugglers cross borders on foot and on mule-back, by cars or by trucks, by fishing boats and luxurious yachts, or use airliners and private planes if the money involved is high, switching from one to another based on the circumstances and the security of the routes. Bewildering combinations of these can be used to avoid law enforcement agencies. Nevertheless, certain routes and ways of transportation do tend to be favoured at different times. For example, until the mid-1990s, human smugglers relied mostly on travelling on foot and by plane. The following years, however, witnessed an increasing number of border crossings by sea as well as on foot. The tendency towards sea transport in particular was a result of increased security measures at borders and airports. The replacement of numerous corrupt security officers in Turkey after concerted efforts undertaken by their agencies as well as the dramatic rise in the number of illegal migrants also played an important role. The most vivid demonstration of the new route was ships sailing up to the coast of Greece and Italy carrying hundreds of illegal migrants. Such ships are highly profitable for human smugglers, who pocket huge sums in a single run. For many desperate migrants they are the only affordable means of entry into Europe. Finally, naval surveillance methods are fully exploited by human smugglers, making the seas a relatively easy route. The trend is also evident in the statistics of Turkey's Central Security Agency. Between 1998 and September 2001, 45 ships which sailed from Turkey were caught abroad, carrying a total of 12,903 illegal migrants. 89 suspects were charged with human smuggling. Of the illegal migrants, 10,426 were caught in Italy and 2,487 in Greece.

While the late-1990s witnessed a decrease in seaborne traffic to Italy, the exact opposite can be observed with regard to Greece. In the first eight months of 2000, three ships took 707 illegal migrants to Greece; in the first eight months of 2001, the numbers increased to nine ships and 2,409 migrants. According to the Greek authorities, 2,172 illegal migrants and 62 human smugglers who sailed from Turkey were caught in the same period. These figures do not include human smuggling carried out in the Aegean with small boats. According to the Central Security Agency, 38 small-scale efforts to reach Greek islands in the Aegean were uncovered between 1997 and September 2001, with 282 migrants and 12 human smugglers caught. Apart from those caught in Italy and Greece, 24 ships and 3,845 illegal migrants were caught in Turkey in the same period. 76 suspects were arrested on charges of human smuggling. In 2000, 29,390 people were caught while waiting to board ships; the same figure for the first eight months of 2001 was 16,654.

The cases below, which come from the media coverage of the incidents, not only reflect the fact that the sea route has been favoured for the smuggling of migrants from Turkey to Greece in the last five years, but also present various features of the smuggling business. In the absence of reliable and comprehensive data on human smuggling from Turkey to

Greece, such media reports offer an interesting, if incidental, snapshot from which to sketch a relatively comprehensive picture of the dynamics and mechanisms of human smuggling over the past five years.

> Greek authorities refuse a cargo ship packed with 380 migrants permission to dock in Greece. After that, the vessel sails around Greek islands for days, crossing in and out of international waters under close surveillance by Greek coast guard vessels. The ship is believed to come from Turkey and is sailing under the false name *Vodelai I*. It has a Bulgarian crew but does not bear a flag. The crew claim migrants on board have commandeered the ship and say water and food is running out. The smugglers apparently reckon Greek authorities will, as has happened many times before, end up by authorizing the migrants to disembark, in order to bring the plight of the passengers to an end. This time, however, the scheme does not work. Highlighting a new determination to seal off overland and sea smuggling routes into Greece, Greek authorities decide to ferry food and drinking supplies to the migrants by helicopter, rather than granting the cargo ship permission to land. On 13 December, the ship is finally allowed to dock in the Italian port of Otranto after nine days at sea. (*FECL* 59, 15 December 1999)

> Six Turkish men accused of transporting 334 illegal immigrants across the Aegean Sea faced smuggling charges on Monday, Greek reports said. The immigrants, including 97 children, said they spent six days at sea in a 30-meter [98-foot] wooden boat before reaching the island of Crete on Sunday. (*TDN*, 8 August 2000)

> Greek authorities continued their search of the Aegean island of Evia on Thursday for more than 100 illegal immigrants from a group of about 350 dropped off from a smuggling boat believed to have sailed from Turkey. A Merchant Marine Ministry official said the coast guard and police had already detained 236 Iraqis, including 13 children, as well as three Turkish smugglers on the large island just off the mainland, northeast of Athens. (*TDN*, 7 September 2001).

> Four illegal immigrants have drowned and several others are feared dead after two smuggling boats were caught in a storm off an island near Athens. Authorities said rescue crews, aided by an all-weather helicopter, were searching for survivors along a remote coastline of the Aegean Sea island of Evia, about 110 km north of Athens. The merchant marine ministry said 95 immigrants – mostly Iraqi Kurds and Afghans – had already been found and placed in temporary

accommodation. Two Turkish smuggling suspects were also arrested. (*Herald Sun*, 20 December 2002).

Dozens of illegal immigrants were rescued from a leaking boat in Turkey's territorial waters following a joint operation yesterday morning by the Greek and Turkish coast guards in the eastern Aegean. Greece's Merchant Marine Ministry said the boat with some 70 passengers was located in Turkish waters near the Greek islet of Farmakonizi following an air and sea search. The operation was launched after a man phoned the coast guard to report a migrant-smuggling ship in distress in the area. Authorities in Turkey were notified, and a Turkish patrol boat safely evacuated all the immigrants. There were no reports concerning their nationality or state of health. (*Kathiremini*, 26 November 2003).

THE CHALLENGE OF IRREGULAR TRANSBORDER MOVEMENTS FOR TURKEY AND GREECE AND REGIONAL CONSEQUENCES

The issue of transborder crime moved to the forefront of official concern in Turkey and Greece in 1999. This was partly because of the emerging Greek–Turkish *rapprochement* (Öniş: 2001) late that year, and partly because of external concerns originating among various regional and neighbouring actors. In that respect, two major regional initiatives were already operational: the Southeastern Europe Cooperation Initiative (SECI)[3] with its regional centre for combating transborder crime, and the EU-initiated Stability Pact for Southeastern Europe[4] with its mechanisms for combating organized crime and strengthening police and border coopration. It was felt that 'drug trafficking, illegal migration, and terrorism are a priority for Greece and Turkey; therefore cooperation in this field was a necessity'.[5]

The main architects of the emerging collaboration between Greece and Turkey were the foreign ministers of these countries, İsmail Cem and Andreas Papandreou. Turkish Foreign Minister Cem sent a letter to his Greek counterpart on 24 May 1999 and invited Papandreou to address with him the problem of perceived links existing in Greece with terrorist organizations. He also suggested that Turkey and Greece conclude an agreement to combat terrorism. The Greek foreign minister responded to Cem's letter on 25 June 1999. While setting forth his views concerning the parameters and modalities of future Turkish–Greek cooperation, Papandreou also conveyed, through the Greek ambassador in Ankara, his wish to meet the Turkish foreign minister in New York on the sidelines of the friends of Kosovo meeting in which both Turkey and Greece were to participate.

It was within the above context that the foreign ministers of Turkey and Greece agreed, in New York on 30 June 1999, to carry out talks at the level of high-ranking diplomatic officers from the respective ministries of foreign affairs to examine possibilities for bilateral cooperation in fields such as the economy, trade, tourism, environment, culture, multilateral cooperation and *combating transborder crime*. All these efforts were exceptionally fruitful, preparing the visits of Papandreou to Ankara in January 2000 and his Turkish counterpart Cem to Athens in February 2000, during which nine agreements were signed. Among them, there was also the Agreement on Combating Crime, Especially Terrorism, Organized Crime, Illicit Drug Trafficking and Illegal Immigration, which came into force on 17 July 2001. Papandreou and Cem also signed a protocol in Athens in November 2001. The protocol provides for cooperation between the Ministry of Public Order of Greece and the Ministry of Interior of Turkey on readmission of citizens of either country or third-country nationals who illegally entered the territory of either Greece or Turkey. The readmission procedure falls under specific rules agreed upon by the two countries, which came into force on 5 August 2002.

Concerns expressed by both Greece and Turkey after the completion of the agreement and the protocol mirrored these countries' differing perspectives which were the results of different views on particular security issues. For instance, the Greek foreign minister seemed to insist that his country would not send back political refugees and along with the Turkish foreign minister agreed that the two countries would work on exchanging information on immigrant-smuggling networks, which he said were often connected with drug and weapons trafficking and terrorist organizations. While the Greek side often implied the sensitivity of the refugee issues, which were directly related to the Kurdish question in Turkey, the Turkish side referred to the assumed Greek support to the separatist Kurdish organization PKK. Although the specific security concerns differed, the authorities of the two countries were quite keen to cooperate in the fight against organized crime, illegal immigration, illicit drug trafficking and terrorism.

According to the agreement, Turkey and Greece commit themselves to cooperate in combating: terrorist activities and crimes committed by individuals or groups; illicit cultivation, production, trade, transportation and abuse of narcotic drugs, psychotropic substances and chemicals used in the production of them; other organized crimes (such as illicit trafficking of persons); illicit trafficking of arms, including biological, chemical and radioactive weapons, ammunition, explosives, nuclear and radioactive materials, as well as poisonous substances; forgery in passports, visas and other official documents; trans-border crimes and criminals; illegal immigration; illicit trafficking of cultural and historical works of art; money laundering; money laundering in relation to one or more of the above mentioned acts, as well as other criminal acts.[6]

As noted earlier, Turkey and Greece are located on the 'southern Balkan Route' along which smugglers move illegal migrants from Asia and Africa into Turkey and Greece and then to western Europe. It is estimated that a maximum of 15–20 per cent of the migrants that enter these two countries remain there, while the rest try to continue to western Europe. Among these migrants, there are those who are not able to move to Europe. However, comparatively only a very small number of illegal migrants stay in Turkey, but many more end up staying in Greece. It appears that there is another route of smuggling, the 'northern Balkan Route' or the 'Istanbul Express', coming from the Middle East, transiting through Turkey, taking a path leading to the EU, via Bulgaria, Romania, Hungary, Slovakia and the Czech Republic.

In short, over the last decade Turkey, Greece and other Balkan countries have been increasingly confronted with large-scale irregular migration, usually in transit to the EU (Di Nicola 1999: 7). This phenomenon has a number of political, social and economic implications, not only for the individual countries, but also for the Balkan region, and the wider context of Europe. Consequently, there have been growing concerns on the issues of irregular migration, smuggling and trafficking issues over the years, in Turkey, Greece and the Balkan countries. This is partly the result of mounting pressure on the countries of transit and origin by the countries of destination in western Europe with the objective to prevent control more effectively the transit of irregular migrants, and to combat the smuggling and trafficking. While the direction of these migrant flows is from east to west and from south to north, the direction of criticism is also from west to east and from south to north.

What has often been achieved at local, national, regional and international level is to agree to strengthen cooperation among participating states in order to combat criminal activities linked to irregular migration, such as trafficking and smuggling in humans. There are also very clear and concrete attempts to institutionalize these cooperation efforts. The already mentioned examples, such as the Southeastern Europe Cooperation Initiative (SECI) with its regional centre for combating transborder crime, and the EU-initiated Stability Pact for Southeastern Europe with its mechanisms for combating organized crime and strengthening police and border cooperation, are the results of these efforts. Another institutionalization effort is certainly the establishment of readmission agreements, as in the case of Turkey and Greece. The importance given to the readmission agreements by the EU is very obvious. For instance, in the Seville conclusions, the European Council 'urge[d] that any future cooperation, association or equivalent agreement which the European Union or the European Community concludes with any country should include a clause on joint management of migration flows and on compulsory readmission in the event of illegal immigration'.[7] More recent meetings of the EU council have put greater emphasis upon these clauses and agreements, often referring to 'Europe's back door' areas such as the Balkans (*The Observer*, 4 February 2001).

The ongoing discussion of illegal migration-related regional problems in Europe and the Balkans often concludes that the spread of illegal migration threatens regional security as it expands region-wide and is connected with regional networks of transborder crime. It is argued that this situation may persist, requiring constant vigilance and preparedness from national, regional and international actors. What was said in the EU–Western Balkans Forum of the JHA Ministerial Meeting in Brussels on 28 November 2003 is an example of this concern: 'Organised crime and corruption are obstacles to democratic stability ... and economic development in the Western Balkans. Particular focus should be placed upon fighting all forms of trafficking, particularly of human beings, drugs and arms, as well as smuggling of goods' (EU Council 2003).

CONCLUDING REMARKS

In conclusion, it is possible to make two main observations based on the analysis of the human smuggling business between Turkey and Greece and its regional consequences. It is possible to claim that these two issues are so utterly dissimilar in nature that is obviously ambitious to attempt to discuss them both in the same brief article. However, I emphasise the need for an evaluation of these issues together as they figure in the transborder crime debate in Balkans in general, and in the case of Turkey and Greece in particular. First, the preceding discussion leaves very little room for doubt about the existence of substantial level of human smuggling from Turkey to Greece, though not in the form of an operation of a massive, centralized, and all-encompassing criminal organization. Second, mostly relying on the findings from the northern and western part of the Balkan region, human trafficking and smuggling in the Balkans is often seen as going hand-in-hand with the organized crime, such as drug and arms trafficking and corruption. Consequently, this perception and understanding of human trafficking and smuggling mostly leads to a whole range of security-dominated measures at governmental, intergovernmental, regional and EU levels. Whether business-like, centralized criminal organizations dominate the human smuggling (and trafficking) in Balkans and its neighbouring regions rather than looser network held together by interest of the individuals operating in the market of these regions, the human smuggling along the Turkey–Greece–Balkans route has caused intensified debate over the last few years on issues such as the fight against organized crime and border management along the Balkans–Europe line.

In the case of Turkish–Greek illegal border crossings, in order to reach an overall understanding of human smuggling, it is imperative for us to realize that smugglers do not always constitute a massive, centralized and all-encompassing criminal organization. Overall, human smuggling between Greece and Turkey is carried out mostly by independent individuals who specialize in relatively narrow fields and unite their efforts through a web of communications and transportation. In this respect, they differ from organizations engaged in drug and arms trafficking, and they do not necessarily have close ties with such organizations. If the human smugglers lack a central organization, how are they able to run their system with an efficiency close to perfection? The answer to this, as illustrated in detail in this article, lies in the employment of several means within the system of smuggling. Advances in technology and global interaction are fully taken advantage of by human smugglers. For example, cellular phones have become a vital component of the migration process, enabling a strong web of communications between and among smugglers but also between smugglers and migrants. Smuggling operations are assisted by the presence of relatives and friends in different parts of the world. For example, a would-be illegal migrant living in Iraq first contacts a friend or relative living in Germany, both to lend him money for the smugglers and to deliver the money to the smugglers in a safe way.

It should be noted that the relationship between the illegal migrant and the smuggler is often solely based on a mutual understanding of trust. As explained above, the smugglers in many cases receive their payments only after having delivered the illegal migrant into his/her country of destination. Likewise, the migrants who experience 'incidents' on their way to the country of destination are guaranteed success in the next attempt, when they are carried to the final point for free. Smugglers can potentially take advantage of illegal migrants in many ways, especially during border crossings. However, the need for mutual trust often results in cordial relationships between the migrants and the smugglers, and incidents of fooling and muscling are rarer than one might expect. Nevertheless, this should not be taken as a sign of the smugglers being humane. Within the overall market relationship, where there is enormous and constant demand from illegal migrants, the smugglers ultimately take full advantage of them. Although mutual trust is needed in order to facilitate human transaction, it does not change the exploitative nature of human smuggling and trafficking.

What this article offers is a partial answer to the question: 'Is there something fundamentally new about the manner in which transnational criminal groups and syndicates operate in the early twenty-first century?" (Berdal and Serrano 2002: 1) with specific reference to human smuggling. The present study emphasises the multidimensional context of irregular border crossings, on the basis of which the nature of the human smuggling should be understood and policy initiatives may be suggested. The emphasis here is on the employment of migrants' networks, human ties and interpersonal trust between smugglers and irregular migrants. An attempt is made to avoid reductionist approaches. This is a reaction against the established dominant criminology-based views on human smuggling. These approaches generally attempt to heighten interest in the subject by focusing on the criminality and security aspects of human smuggling. Certainly 'security' and 'criminality' aspects are present in human smuggling, but I feel that these limited perspectives are reductionist in addressing the complexity of this particular phenomenon. The multidimensional context of human smuggling can be systematically addressed if migration networks and the human ties between smugglers and irregular migrants are considered alongside the 'security' and 'criminality' aspects. When combating human smuggling, this multidimensional nature is not something that policy makers should ignore.

Something else that policy makers should also consider is that there is a need for burden sharing, rather than burden shifting, between countries. Today not only Turkey and Greece, but also countries in the Balkans and Europe, face many challenges in relation to the management and control of irregular migration flows into them. As it is discussed above, the countries in the relative-west, in particular, are greatly concerned over irregular migration flows through the countries in the relative-east. This presents the countries in the relative-east with a dilemma. On the one hand, the countries in the relative-east are under pressure from the countries in the relative-west to improve their control mechanisms and law enforcement capabilities to combat and limit the flow of illegal migrants. On the other, the countries in the relative-east cannot realistically be expected to comply with such demands without the necessary resources and assistance. Therefore, there is a need for burden-sharing between the countries of the relative-east and those of the relative-west, especially in relation to a phenomenon like irregular transit migration that ultimately targets western European countries.

NOTES

1. Since 1999 the Maritime Safety Committee of the IMO has established a recording and reporting system to keep track of incidents of unsafe practices associated with the trafficking or transport of illegal migrants by sea. Results of this system have been tabulated and disseminated by IMO.
2. The European police agency Europol often declares that criminal gangs now make as much from smuggling humans as they do from drugs.
3. The participating states of the Southeast European Cooperative Initiative (SECI) held an inaugural meeting in Geneva on 5–6 December 1996 and formally adopted the SECI Statement of Purpose on 6 December 1996. The thinking behind SECI is to encourage cooperation among its participating states and to facilitate their integration into European structures. SECI is not an assistance programme. It does not interfere with, but rather complements, existing initiatives. SECI endeavours to promote close cooperation between and among the governments of the region and to create new channels of communication between and among them.
4. On 10 June 1999, at the EU's initiative, the Stability Pact for South Eastern Europe was adopted in Cologne. In the founding document, more than 40 partner countries and organizations undertook to strengthen the countries of South Eastern Europe 'in their efforts to foster peace, democracy, respect for human rights and economic prosperity in order to achieve stability in the whole region'.
5. See letter from George Papandreou, foreign minister of the Republic of Greece, to İsmail Cem, foreign minister of the Republic of Turkey, 25 June 1999, ⟨www.greekturkish.forum.org/docu_c2.htm⟩.
6. See Article 1 of the Agreement between the Republic of Turkey and the Hellenic Republic on Cooperation of the Ministry of Internal Affairs of the Republic of Turkey and the Ministry of Public Order of the Hellenic Republic on Combating Crime, Especially Terrorism, Organized Crime, Illicit Drug Trafficking and Illegal Immigration.
7. See ⟨http://europa.eu.int/comm/seville_council/index_en.html⟩.

REFERENCES

Berdal, Mats and Monica Serrano, eds (2002): *Transnational Organised Crime and International Security.* Boulder and London: Lynne Rienner.
BFBA (2001a): *Documents and Views on Foreigners, Borders, and Asylum, 2000.* Ankara: Ministry of Interior, Bureau for Foreigners, Borders and Asylum.
BFBA (2001b): *Illegal Migration around the World and Turkey.* Ankara: Ministry of Interior, Bureau for Foreigners, Borders and Asylum.
Di Nicola, Andrea (1999): 'Trafficking in Immigrants: A European Perspective', paper presented at the Colloquium on Cross-border Crime in Europe, Prague, 27–28 September.
EU Council (2003): *Joint Conclusions, EU–Western Balkans Forum, JHA Ministerial Meeting, Brussels, 28 November 2003* (SN 3559/1/03, REV1).
İçduygu, Ahmet (2003a): *Irregular Migration in Turkey*, Geneva: International Organization on Migration.
İçduygu, Ahmet (2003b): 'SOPEMI Report for Turkey', paper presented to the OECD Meeting of the SOPEMI Correspondents, Paris, 10–12 December
İçduygu, Ahmet and Şule Toktaş (2002): 'How Do Smuggling and Trafficking Operate via Irregular Border Crossings in the Middle East? Evidence from Fieldwork in Turkey', *International Migration*, 40:6, pp.25–54.
Jordan, Bill and Franck Düvell (2003): *Migration, The Boundaries of Equality and Justice.* Cambridge: Polity.
King, Russell (1998): 'The Mediterranean: Europe's Rio Grande', in Malcolm Anderson and Eberhard Bort, eds, *The Frontiers of Europe.* London and Washington: Pinter.

Kollias, Christos and Gülay Günlük-Şenesen, eds (2003): *Greece and Turkey in the 21st Century: Conflict or Cooperation.* New York: Nova Science Publishers.

Öniş, Ziya (2001): 'Greek–Turkish Relations and the European Union: A Crucial Perspective', *Mediterranean Politics,* 6:3, pp.31–45.

Papadopoulou, Aspasia (2002): 'Kurdish Asylum Seekers in Greece: the Role of Networks in the Migration Process', paper presented at the UNU/WIDER Conference on Poverty, International Migration and Asylum, Helsinki, 27–28 September.

Salt, John (2000): 'Trafficking and Human Smuggling: a European Perspective', *International Migration,* 38:3, pp.31–56.

Yılmaz, Abdurrahman (2003): 'Edirne'den Gelişmiş Ülkelere Gitme Teşebbüsünde Bulunan Transit Göçmenler' [Those Transit Migrants who Have Intention of Moving from Edirne to the Developed Countries], unpublished PhD dissertation, Yeditepe University, Istanbul.

Anti-Corruption and Anti-Organized Crime Policy in Serbia: Regional Implications

ALEKSANDAR FATIĆ

LEGISLATIVE, TRAINING AND INSTITUTIONAL REFORM ISSUES TIED TO CORRUPTION AND ORGANISED CRIME

Much of the effort of the former Serbian government (2001–2004) was dedicated to the struggle against corruption and organized crime, which were perceived as premier threats to the country's internal security and economic well being. It is to be expected that the new government, which came into power in 2004, will continue along much the same agenda of priorities, where fighting corruption will remain high on the list of problems to be addressed. This is the result of a longer-term overhaul of the predominant conceptualization of security in the whole region of southeast Europe (SEE). Notions of conventional 'hard' or military security are giving way to the new concept of 'soft', predominantly internal security. Security threats do not come from antagonistic foreign states, but from antagonistic actors within the system itself, namely from organized criminal groups, systemic corruption and the longitudinal processes of creation of systemic inadequacies that threaten the economic well being of society in the long term. This trend has nowhere been more emphasised than in Serbia, where in 2003 the reformist prime minister, Dr Zoran Đinđić, was assassinated in front of the government building, triggering the most massive anti-organized crime operation in the history of the Serbian police, codenamed 'Sable'. The operation led to over 8,000 arrests and evidence to suggest that major chains of corruption related to the drugs trade, mixed with political motives to avoid the International Criminal Tribunal for the Former Yugoslavia-related extraditions, had been behind the assassination. This has highlighted just how intimately violent forms of organized crime are connected with systemic corruption. According to police statements, at least two members of the State Security Service *(Bezbednosno-informativna agencija – BIA)* were involved, as well as several members of the former elite security unit, the infamous Special Operations Unit *(Jedinica za specijalne operacije – JSO)*.

Serbia has a legacy of systemic inadequacies as a result of the actions of the former government before the democratic changes in 2000. Perhaps the most obvious mismanagement of public affairs occurred through the massive draining away of public funds through inflated exchange rates, synergies between the state banks and street dealers of 'black' currency, and the total lack of transparency of financial and budgeting procedures in the previous period. Against this background, since the 'democratic revolution' in October 2000, the government has systematically introduced measures to curb corruption in the public sector and provide systemic responses to the systemic inadequacies created by the previous regime. First, the new government recognized that there was in fact organized crime in Serbia (something that the previous regime had been reluctant to even admit). Then it proceeded to introduce specific structures within the police force, the financial control structures, and the other relevant parts of the public administration system to address the identified problems. Clearly, the first step in the corruption-control effort had to be an overhaul of criminal legislation, which up to 2000 did not even mention the word 'corruption' and did not sanction corruption as a criminal offence in any explicit way.

Many of the offences that could generally be considered as falling under the heading of corruption could be sanctioned under different articles of the Serbian Criminal Law, namely under 'abuse of official position", which allowed the effective prosecution of all those who have abused public funds in one way or another. However, a large part of the spectrum of corruption was left uncovered by this offence, as corruption not only included the abuse of public funds, but also numerous actions or inactions, taken in an official capacity, that could benefit the perpetrator or other persons, and that were not motivated by the legitimate public interest and were not executed in accordance with the law and public authorisations.

In 2001, officials of the Serbian Ministry of Justice approached the Management Centre, an NGO based in Beograd that specializes in anti-corruption training and policy design, to request assistance in designing a new Law Against Organized Crime and Corruption. At that time, in coop-eration with the Netherlands government, the Management Centre had already started a year-long project on designing a comprehensive Law Against Organized Crime. However, the Serbian Ministry of Justice requested such a law to be finished 'within a few weeks', an impossible task, given that this was to be a special law, including very complicated procedural, material and penal provisions. All these had to be both differ-ent from the existing provisions in the systemic legislation, and suffi-ciently compatible with existing solutions so as not to create serious disturbances within the legal system. Following a high level discussion on this issue, a compromise solution was struck. The joint team of the Minis-try of Justice and the Management Centre would work on amendments to the then current criminal law to include anti-corruption provisions. The solutions envisaged by the Management Centre in the comprehensive Law Against Organised Crime and Corruption would be taken into account in a more comprehensive legislative effort to regulate this area during the course of the following two years.

The result of the above developments was an overhauled Serbian Criminal Law, with an added entire chapter, Chapter 21A – Criminal Offences of Corruption, which now consists of nine new incriminations, including:

- Corruption in the Public Administration (Article 255a);
- Mismanagement of the Public Funds (Article 255b);
- Corruption in Public Procurement (Article 255v);
- Corruption in the Privatisation Process (Article 255g);
- Corruption in the Judiciary (Article 255d);
- Abuse of the Function of Attorney (Article 255dj);
- Corruption in the Health Services (Article 255e);
- Corruption in the Education System (Article 255zh); and
- Setting up of the Outcome of a Sports Match (Article 255z).

These new incriminations have made it possible for the prosecution to address specific corruption cases more directly and effectively, yet it is still too early to tell just how effective the legislation will be in practice. The entire process of drafting the new legislation demonstrated serious deficiencies in the criminal justice system. Due to pressures coming from interest groups, it proved difficult to include additional offences of corruption in relation to attorneys' activities, corruption of judges, etc. As a result, the new Serbian Criminal Law penalizes, for example, the taking of bribes by schoolteachers with three to five years imprisonment. According to the Serbian criminal justice system all those offences for which the minimum sentence provided for is three years cannot be sanctioned by probation. Consequently, a school teacher who, as a result of the general atmosphere of corruption, might have taken a present or a bribe, will go to prison for three years, if convicted, though he or she may have had no previous convictions. By contrast, an attorney who deliberately misleads the court to the advantage or, as is sometimes the case, to the disadvantage of his or her client, is not effectively penalized.

In addition, the pressure exerted by the Management Centre representatives resulted in the final abolition of the death penalty from the Serbian Criminal Law. On the other hand, government representatives insisted on systematically increasing the penalties for practically all other offences. This has resulted in a serious inbalance in the value-system of the entire penal policy. While the death penalty has been abolished for the most serious offences, penalties for minor offences, which were already quite substantial, have been increased.

The changes introduced in the Serbian Criminal Law are important, and they mark a milestone in the development of the Serbian Criminal Justice System, yet they are insufficient and suffer from serious internal contradictions. Further reform of the Serbian political system, and of the Ministry of Justice in particular, is necessary in order to improve criminal justice legislation. Of course, implementing the anti-corruption policy has also to do with the position of the courts in the Serbian criminal justice system. At the moment, the judiciary is considerably sidelined as until recently it was in conflict with the executive government, and major restructuring of the judiciary is underway by the executive arm of the government. This is an unfortunate and strange situation from the point of view of the principle of separation of powers as a fundamental principle of democracy, but a politically influenced and dysfunctional judiciary has made it necessary for the government to initiate major reforms in this sector.

All these changes of legislation indicate a piecemeal approach to reforms. Furthermore, it appears difficult to introduce long-lasting legislative reforms. The frequent changes of legislation cause two negative consequences. First, they make it difficult for the prosecution and the courts to fully understand and implement the laws. Second, they undermine public trust in institutions, since the institutions change the laws in response to every major crisis in the country.

In addition to the new criminal legislation, the Serbian government introduced the new Law on Public Procurements and established a Directorate for Public Procurements within the Ministry of Finance. This directorate is charged with monitoring all public procurement procedures and ensuring that they are transparent and conducted in a fair and legal way. Simultaneously, the Serbian Ministry of Finance established a special Anti-Corruption Section, whose members have undergone specialized training in anti-corruption methodology conducted by the Management Centre, in cooperation with the Canadian government. The Customs Directorate has established a special Anti-Smuggling Squad, whose members have also undergone the same training.

The Serbian Ministry of the Interior established a special Anti-Organized Crime Directorate, which has already demonstrated its capacity to effectively attack organized crime. The members of the Anti-Organized Crime Directorate have undergone a specialist course in the modern methodology to fight organized crime. This is organized by the Security Policy Group of the Management Centre, in cooperation with the United States Institute of Peace, and the programme is continuing in cooperation with the Netherlands government.

The democratic changes as of October 2000 have also led to serious cuts into the traditional and largely conservative tissue of the Serbian Police Force, which had been blamed for serious violations of the law and of their own internal rules and decisions during the period when they had acted virtually as the Praetorian Guard for the former Communist regime. During the past few years they have undergone structural adjustments. Due to various international influences and expert advice received from local experts, primarily filtered through the Serbian government as a whole, they have emerged as a new structure, with specialized units and forces intended for quick action to address the most burning issues, including corruption and organized crime.

Generally speaking, the concept of organized crime as adopted by the Serbian Ministry of the Interior, and as viewed by the Serbian government more generally, is inclusive of corruption. Understanding corruption as an element and, in some cases, as a precondition for the operation of organized criminal syndicates is integral to understanding the way in which Serbian society is attempting to fight both problems. This is why it is difficult to discuss the policies against these two phenomena entirely separately, as they are interwoven substantially at all levels of policy implementation.

KEY METHODS TO FIGHT CORRUPTION WITH SPECIAL REGARD TO SERBIAN CIRCUMSTANCES

The first general strategy to be applied in fighting corruption in the entire region of Southeast Europe, and specifically in Serbia, is to create structures that will by-pass the corrupt parts of the public administration system. This is a system of specialized police units and other control agencies, including the special sections of the Financial Police, which will have direct lines of responsibility to individuals in high office. This strategy is well tried in central European countries. One of the most striking examples of the efficacy of such an approach is that of the Czech Republic, where a special anti-corruption and anti-organized crime police structure was created in the early 1990s, at an early stage of the social and political transition, which was directly responsible to the prime minister. Only months after its creation, this unit arrested the then director of the government's Agency for Privatization, Jaroslav Lizner, in a night club in Prague with a suitcase full of money. Later Lizner was sacked and became the first high-level-corruption-related prisoner in central Europe. The strategy to introduce such special lines of responsibility of control agencies that would circumvent the conventional hierarchy of the system is underway in Serbia, although rather shyly and with many obstructions from various quarters.

The second general strategy is the creation of special parliamentary committees for the oversight of anti-corruption policy. This is still an idea in the making. Such moves have been tried at the level of the executive government, which recently created an Anti-Corruption Council, the work of which has been marred by lack of cooperation by the government, and by internal strife. Several members of the council have resigned so far, and the results of the council generally speaking are poor. Indeed not a single anti-corruption law was adopted in the year called 'The Anti-Corruption Year'. In fact, this was the reason for the resignation of a high-positioned member of the council, Čedomir Čupić, in February 2003. The creation of special *parliamentary* committees is going to be difficult because traditionally such committees are supposed to have an opposition chairmanship. However, the current parliamentary opposition in Serbia includes the former Miločević regime members, whose credentials are such that the public has no trust at all in their value as an anti-corruption body.

The third pillar of anti-corruption policy is the structural reorganization of the entire system of public administration, primarily through the re-positioning of experts in the system. Namely, this strategy means that an expert body should be created to act as a coordinator between all the stake-holders in the anti-corruption and the public administration reform policy. In such a scenario all or most of the interactions between the various traditional systemic actors would be channelled through a central expert body, which would serve as a filter for ideas and policies.

The implementation of most policies depends on foreign economic assistance, given that almost the entire development of Serbia is aid driven at the moment. To maintain a transparent public administration system and a durable system of oversight of the integrity of the entire public life in Serbia, the role of international partners, and especially the international donors, is essential.[1]

The fourth pillar of anti-corruption policy in Serbia concerns donor policy. It is imperative to preserve the polycentric donor policy and bilateral donor–recipient relationships at any price, and avoid the pitfalls of so-called 'administrative coordination' by international organizations, as it is well established that such 'coordination' is the rockbed of possible misuse and corruption. One of the greatest dangers is that the constituencies of the large western-European democracies might develop a scepticism towards assisting the transition effort in Serbia and other Balkan countries due to the problems arising from corrupt, locally entrenched international bureaucracies, which tend to develop kickback-type relationships with the local elites, and 'coordinate' the aid provided by western donors in ways known only to the local bureaucrats. To give an example: UNDP, the most obvious example of such 'coordination', collected funds from bilateral donors for the so-called 'capacity-building' of the government. It is conceivable that the funds provided by bilateral donors might be used by UNDP bureaucrats to stimulate local elites whose members travelled around the European capitals and 'praised the good work' of those same locally entrenched bureaucrats. This may stifle real reform in Serbia where independent actors have been and remain the central forces that keep the public institutions and the entire transition process on track through their ideas, platforms, expertise, integrity and checks that they perform on the work of the government. Depriving those traditional and well-tried partners of aid in favour of international bureaucracies risks resulting in corruption at the centralized level of such aid coordination. Empirical results in other countries of the region confirm this assumption. More institutionally speaking, international organizations involved in development aid ought to be systematically discouraged from establishing local offices with any discretionary authorizations. This has proven to be a recipe for corruption through the local entrenchment of structures with embedded personal and group interests, yet endowed with resources that are not their own.[2]

The fifth method to fight corruption envisaged by the Serbian government has been the criminalization of corruption in as many incriminations in the criminal legislation as possible. (At the beginning of this article I spoke about certain things that have been achieved in this regard). Once the executive, judiciary and legislative bodies are adequately reformed, more remains to be done in a more systematic and sound way, for instance further work on Serbian criminal legislation.

The sixth method includes the introduction of special anti-corruption legislation, and such legislation has been partially introduced through the special Law on the Special Authorizations of State Organs in Fighting Organized Crime, although this is not the same as a special anti-corruption law. An Anti-Corruption Law has in fact been prepared by the Management Centre, and sent to the government, and it now remains to be seen whether such a law will be enacted. Part of the dissatisfaction by the government's only Anti-Corruption Council stems from the fact that this and other related laws have not yet been adopted, although they had long been announced and various officials openly admit that there is a need for them.

The sixth step involves the enacting of a Law on the Conflict of Interest. This Law, long worked on by the expert community, was announced in Winter 2003 by the Ministry of Finance and Economy, and it is expected that it will soon be enacted. However, the change of government in 2004 leaves it uncertain whether the new government will wish to include new provisions in the draft, which could further delay enactment of the law.[3]

Seventh, a Law on Public Access to Information is key to enabling the transparent oversight of the work of public administration. According to official announcements, this law is also in the process of being drafted, while several expert organizations have already prepared their drafts.

Eighth, the process of appointment of public functionaries is still conducted in ways that are neither democratic nor transparent. These appointees are not political appointees, and they ought to be appointed through open competitions on the basis of the quality of candidates in the way that is adopted in all European democracies. For some reason, in Serbia even those appointments are still held strictly in secret and made behind closed doors. Moves are underway amongst the professional public in Serbia to address this anachronism and make sure that the personnel policy in the professional services is professional and competitive.

Much of the anti-corruption policy in Serbia, as indeed anti-corruption policies in most other countries in SEE, is based on western European experiences, including the experiences of the former Yugoslav countries that are in the 'first tier' of candidature for EU membership. On one level, this demonstrates a natural kinship of policies between and among the Yugoslav successor states, given the largely shared pool of corruption-related problems, partly arising from their experience of political and economic transition. On another level, this demonstrates the tendency to copy the policies of the countries close by, while being more reserved to the experiences of more remote regions. For example, work on the Law on the Anti-Corruption Agency, which is underway in Serbia now, is largely geared by the experiences of the Slovenian Anti-Corruption Office. The main concept seems to be to establish an agency which would not have repressive authority, and which would basically engage in academic and analytic work, comparing and developing legislation and policy. However, the latest reports by the Council of Europe on the performance of Slovenian anti-corruption policy have been rather critical, and have in fact mentioned the need to condition the Slovenian EU accession process by its more effective performance in the building up of institutions for corruption control. The Slovenian Anti-Corruption Office has, in other words, proven rather ineffective. Therefore Serbia, as well as the other SEE countries, perhaps needs to look farther away from their neighbourhood for successful corruption control examples. The so-called Singapore–Hong-Kong model has proven highly successful, and has brought Hong Kong to the very top of the countries fighting corruption, measured by the effects of their anti-corruption policies.

CONCLUSION

In Serbia corruption and organized crime are very closely linked. This makes it necessary to develop a consolidated set of anti-corruption and anti-organized crime policies that go along with the enactment of new legislation and the training of personnel who will be directly involved in the implementation of the proposed policies. Serbian society is presented with the challenge to continue along the path of implementing the legislative reforms – briefly presented in this article – but also promoting institutional and organizational reforms. To this end the role of experts is very important. Most of the existing anti-crime and anti-corruption policies and moves by the Serbian government have been prepared and assisted by experts' think-tanks. The pace and success of the reform initiative considerably depend on international partners. This is the right time for international development aid to flow into Serbia to assist reform efforts. However, it is crucial that it is given to those agents who have a record in preparing the ground for reforms and that it is monitored in a way that leaves no room for corruption by the local distribution centres.

NOTES

1. This article deals with Serbia; however, most of the principles and policies discussed are also either contemplated or being implemented in the other countries of southeast Europe, which means that most of the contents of this article apply equally to the entire region of southeast Europe. The region shares strong similarities in the problems and the possible avenues to remedy those problems, so it is not surprising that most of what can be said of one country could also be said of its neighbours in the Balkans. This applies to the anti-corruption and crime-control policy especially, and even more sharply to the links between corruption and organized crime, which characterize the region so strikingly at the moment.

2. Recently, the Parliament of Sweden has debated the possible abolition of development aid to the region due to abuse, and sensitivities are being alerted there to the fact that the bulk of this abuse emanates from the international administrative structures. This author has been involved in discussions to make sure that it is understood that bilateral relations between Sweden and Serbia and Montenegro are fruitful and that Swedish development aid is disbursed through the most appropriate channels through the Swedish Agency for International Development (SIDA), while problems arise in multilateral organizations trying to 'mediate', where the reservations by the Swedish local representatives towards such 'mediation' are fully justified, and are founded on the possibilities for corrupt and intransparent decision making by the 'mediators'. The same applies to the aid provided by other European countries. Aid can drive certain phases of development in transitional societies, but not the entire process, and only insofar as it is provided to the right actors, directly by the donors, not to overarching structures by mediating agents. The latter is a strategy that wastes the money of the European taxpayers and does not help the target countries and their societies.

3. See 'Šta treba da sadrži Zakon o sprečavanju sukoba interesa' ('How should a Law on the Conflict of Interest Look?'), (*The Pulse*, December 2002–January 2003), The Management Centre, Beograd: 18–22 (A4). This paper contains the entire draft of a structure and general provisions of a modern Law on the Conflict of Interest that would be appropriate to Serbian circumstances. It was prepared by experts of the Management Centre in cooperation with the Dutch government during 2002.

The Role of Civil Society in Fighting Corruption and Organized Crime in Southeast Europe

PLAMEN RALCHEV

After 1990, the global trend towards democracy set a pattern for civil society in southeast Europe (SEE) as a 'hub' for freethinkers and reformers. Before considering the civil society 'input' in fighting corruption and organized crime throughout the region, it is worth highlighting some of the specific features of civil society development in SEE.

GENERAL OVERVIEW OF THE CIVIL SOCIETY SECTOR IN SEE

Civil societies in SEE are heterogeneous and multi-speed and rarely share any common features apart from the functions that civil society organizations are usually supposed to perform. This is partly due to the fact that, following the collapse of the communist systems in the late 1980s, the democratic transition did not start simultaneously in all SEE countries. Furthermore, these countries have inherited different civic cultures from the past. Nonetheless, it is clear that civil societies in SEE countries are developing in terms of organization and capacity, even though they may be developing at different speeds.

The newly emerged civil society organizations started playing an important role in engaging the public in policy dialogue and developing the habits of active civic participation. Non-governmental organizations (NGOs) provide opportunities for addressing important social problems, relieve the state of some of its functions, attract additional resources into the country, create additional opportunities for professional and personal accomplishment.

NON-GOVERNMENT ORGANIZATIONS AS ORGANIZED FORMS OF CIVIL SOCIETY

Civil society is often described as a return to reciprocity in political and social arrangements, and as the third force through which the traditional hierarchy of state and subject can be unseated. The term is used somewhat more rigorously by political scientists to encompass all those substances of society, and all those arrangements within it, that exist outside the state's reach or instigation. But nowadays the most widespread understanding of civil society is as the promoter for a range of political and social goals. In short, civil society has come, simultaneously, to be thought of as encompassing everything that is not the state and as representing a set of inherently democratic values (Triffanova 2003).

The term *NGO* is very broad and encompasses many different types of organizations. In the field of development they include research institutes, churches, professional associations and lobby groups. The World Bank classified two main categories of NGOs: *operational* NGOs, whose primary purpose is the design and implementation of development-related projects; and *advocacy* NGOs, whose primary purpose is to defend or promote a specific cause and who seek to influence the policies and practices (World Bank 1999).

It should be noted, however, that these two categories are not mutually exclusive. A growing number of NGOs engage in both operational and advocacy activities, and some advocacy groups, while not directly involved in designing and implementing projects, focus on specific project-related concerns.

NGO–GOVERNMENT RELATIONSHIPS

The following features of the present operational environment in SEE are considered to bring opportunities to the development of the NGO sector:

basic democratic structures and the willingness of governments to cooperate with civil society actors. NGOs are also assisted by enhanced structural reform in industry, changed societal attitudes to market-economy processes, limitations put on the grey economy, and attraction of foreign investors. However, these features are mostly observable on a macro level and still do not have real influence on people's everyday life. A number of challenges also exist: institutions are weak and there is heavy reform agenda, but in some areas there is no capacity to carry it out. Above all, corruption is a serious problem (Lessenski 2003).

NGOs have proved to be an important and needed part of society. Governments have gradually learned to be tolerant of them and recently have even taken the initiative to use their expertise. The most recent example of the government's changing attitudes toward the NGO sector was the formation in Bulgaria of a parliamentary committee that addresses the problems of civil society. The public council of this commission includes 21 members representing 28 NGOs. Other parliamentary committees recruit NGO experts as advisers when they organize public hearings on issues of national importance. Most governmental officials, however, still retain some hostility toward NGOs (Lessenski and Vassileva 2003).

On the local level, NGOs usually cooperate well with local authorities and media. They understand that NGOs provide very useful resources for policy development in terms of volunteers, expertise, information and links to specific communities. There are examples of NGOs helping policy development with respect to EU accession, as well as training government servants in fields such as working with civil society groups, dealing with concrete local issues, etc. Generally, it is at the level of local government where best examples and good practices of cooperation with NGOs have been recently reported. Local authorities seem to be more open to working with NGOs. However, yet more efforts are needed to transform this type of communication and cooperation into an institutionalized sustainable form of local development.

All these examples outline a positive trend in NGO sector development of raising the level of participation of NGOs in decision making and policy implementation at local and national level.

INVOLVEMENT OF NGOS IN ANTI-CORRUPTION ACTIVITIES

NGOs in SEE are still in a process of defining their fields of interest and special role among a wide range of transition priorities and problems. Anti-corruption, as a relatively novel priority in public agenda, is one of the topics which involve a growing number of NGOs. This involvement is facilitated by the fact that anti-corruption projects increasingly attract the attention of potential western donor organizations (both international bodies and national agencies).

The involvement of NGOs from SEE countries in anti-corruption activities is conditional to three mutual related processes (Centre for Study of Democracy 2002):

1. developments within the third sector in each country;
2. the availability of foreign funds; and
3. the prevailing attitudes of national authorities vis-à-vis anti-corruption efforts by civil society.

Most of anti-corruption activities conducted in SEE were developed as top-down initiatives. Work undertaken is channelled in three dimensions: raising public awareness, providing analyses and recommendation, and training through seminars, workshops and lectures.

Throughout the region local chapters of Transparency International function quite effectively. They are involved not only in monitoring corruption practices but also in proposing and drafting indispensable legislation in different countries. There are also national NGOs that cooperate with Transparency International or establish separate coalitions of like-minded NGOs that conduct monitoring, evaluation and assessment of corruption practices, public perceptions of corruption and propose anti-corruption measures to national authorities.

One of the particular outputs of NGOs' efforts in fighting corruption is the establishment of partnerships between the public and private sector to analyse the causes of corruption and to counteract them effectively.

Generally, in all the countries of the region, first steps were made towards successful anti-corruption cooperation between the executive and non-governmental organizations. However, at the present stage, public–private partnership in this area still tends to be of a sporadic nature and largely depends on the good will of the respective ministers and their teams. Within the third sector itself an even more pronounced emphasis was put on the preventive function of civil society in addition to the awareness-raising component, which was the initial focus of anti-corruption efforts. Thus a number of projects of NGOs are aimed at establishing specific mechanisms of private–public partnership for curbing corrupt practices in various sectors of social life.

Apart from the local chapters of Transparency International, there are also active national NGOs working on the corruption issues either alone or in partnership with other NGOs, representatives of various state institutions and independent experts. In the case of Bulgaria, such concerted efforts are represented by Coalition 2000, which determines to certain extent the shape and nature of civic participation in counteracting corruption (⟨www.transparency.org⟩; ⟨www.transparency-bg.org⟩).

The major areas of civil society's activities for countering corruption include civic monitoring of corruption through regular publishing of Corruption Perception Indexes, anti-corruption public awareness campaigns, consulting and expertise-sharing, anti-corruption education courses, and anti-corruption initiatives both on national and local (munic-ipal) level. Exercising civic control and providing independent expert assistance in such crucial areas as economic and social reforms, privatiza-tion, public tenders and procurement is a substantial contribution of the civil society organizations in fighting corruption.

CIVIL SOCIETY AND ORGANIZED CRIME

Unlike countering corruption, the capacity of civil society to fight orga-nized crime is quite limited, for obvious reasons. Yet there is room for civic efforts to mobilize and foster factors that could, if not eliminate, at least limit organized crime activities.

Major areas where civil society under the form of NGOs has a vital role to play in the fight against organized crime are raising public awareness, informing the general public and influencing public attitudes; conducting research and analysis on issues inter-related with organized crime; and cooperating with state institutions in charge of combating organized crime. In all the countries throughout SEE there are NGOs dedicating their missions and activities to raising public awareness towards sensitive issues connected with organized crime such as drug trafficking, money laundering, trafficking of women and prostitution.

These efforts of the NGO community in SEE have been largely supported by international organizations and foreign state agencies. It is worth mentioning the initiative launched under the auspices of the Inter-national Organization for Migration for Preventing Trafficking in Women in SEE. It turned into one of the success stories of a campaign carried region-wide for preventing one of the fuelling channels for organized crime, namely forced prostitution.

Numerous examples could be cited within the second dimension of NGOs' contribution to fighting organized crime. It directly translates into the capacity developed and expertise acquired by those profiled NGOs that operate either as independent think tanks (policy research institutes) or as resource centres. In each SEE country there are NGOs specialized in studying a wide range of security issues and organized crime in particular. Research and analyses conducted by these NGOs and free dissemination of these data help the general public to form and adhere to common positions and help the respective institutions concerned to shape and pursue proper policies aimed at combating organized crime.

The analytical capacity of NGOs provides for one of the points of interaction between NGOs and state institutions in charge of combating organized crime. Utilizing this capacity and embarking on joint initiatives and projects with NGOs make state institutions more capable of fulfilling their mission and performing their duties more effectively. Therefore, interaction and cooperation between NGOs and state agencies on issues concerning organized crime ultimately improves the expertise, increases the spectrum of policy options and creates a stable environment of partnership, which would make the fight against organized crime as comprehensive as possible.

CIVIL SOCIETY, NGOS AND THE MEDIA

While discussing the role of civil society in fighting corruption and organized crime, it should be stressed that the media are an important partner for optimizing the results. The media and particularly investigative journalists are strategic allies for NGOs working either on anti-corruption initiatives or researching organized crime.

Political pressure on journalists, and especially on media editorial staff, still persists. Nevertheless, throughout the past few years the media and above all independent newspapers in a number of SEE countries have developed a strong interest in investigating and revealing corruption scandals and organized crime activities, sometimes even involving public figures. The public debate, which takes place in and through the independent media, is largely perceived as an expression of civic interest (Centre for Study of Democracy 2002).

POLICY RECOMMENDATIONS

The role of civil society organizations in fighting corruption and organized crime in SEE should be steadily sustained by means of dedicated efforts to improve the standing and performance of these organized forms of civic activism. What is of utmost importance ismaintaining the citizens' vigilance and sensitivity towards criminal activities. This directly calls for raising the public profile of the NGO sector.

In addition, further work is needed in order to institutionalize and develop NGO–government communication and cooperation. There is also a need for tailored training programmes that meet individual

NGOs' organizational capacity needs and encourage constituency building. Further work is necessary for community development and citizen mobilization.

CONCLUSION

Civil societies in SEE countries, though not mature, are vibrant and will develop their potential in the years to come. Civic organizations, as instigators and promoters of civil society development, have a proven record of making societies sensitive to such detrimental factors as corruption and organized crime. Maintaining public awareness is based on providing for an informed public debate on these issues. Therefore, civil society organizations have a pivotal role in fighting corruption and organized crime by keeping the public and the authorities alert and by assisting state authorities in devising approaches to counter corruption and organized crime.

REFERENCES

Centre for Study of Democracy (2002): *Anti-Corruption in Southeastern Europe: First Steps and Policies*; Center for the Study of Democracy. Sofia: Centre for Study of Democracy. Available at ⟨http://www.csd.bg/fileSrc.php?id=10810⟩.
Lessenski, M. (2003): *Civil Society in Southeast Europe*, 2003, IRIS Working. Sofia: Institute for Research in International Studies.
Lessenski, M. G. Vassileva (2003): *NGO Sector Development in Bulgaria*, IRIS Working Paper. Sofia: Institute for Research in International Studies.
Triffonova, E. (2003a): *Civil Society in Southeastern Europe*. Sofia: Institute for Research in International Studies. Available at ⟨http://www.iris-bg.org/publications⟩.
Triffonova, E. (2003b): *Civil Society – Key Element of Post-Cold War Zeitgeist* Sofia: Institute for Research in International Studies. Available at ⟨http://www.iris-bg.org/publications⟩.
World Bank (1999): *NGO-World Bank Collaboration*. Washington, DC: World Bank. Available at ⟨http://www.worldbank.org⟩.

ELIAMEP's Forum on New Security Issues (FONSI): 'Shared Interests & Values between Southeastern Europe & The Transatlantic Community'

WORKSHOP ON 'ENHANCING COOPERATION AGAINST TRANSBORDER CRIME IN SOUTHEAST EUROPE: WHAT ARE THE PRIORITIES?', 28 FEB – 2 MARCH 2003, SOFIA[1]

EXECUTIVE SUMMARY

Rapporteur: Ekavi Athanassopoulou

Major Conclusions

- In order to successfully fight organized crime we need to fully understand its origins and analyse them in detail. The rise of organized crime in southeast Europe (SEE) is directly related to the collapse of the established economic, political and social order during the Communist period and the clash between the old and new economic, political and social reality. It is also directly related to the ethnic conflicts, the embargos imposed by the international community and the presence of foreign troops in SEE. Poverty and unemployment, but also major differences in economic and social status within the same society, further encourage criminal activities.
- In the fight against organized crime it is important to understand that there may be crime which is situational or even 'inevitable'. In other words, in an environment often characterized by the absence of rules and regulations which can facilitate the security and growth of business we can talk about 'inevitable' crime (of course with caution), in cases when without breaking the law individual entepreneurship could be stifled. Also, the definition of what constitutes criminal activity differs according to cultural differences. Our capacity to understand organized

crime in SEE needs to be based on a cultural understanding of the societies in this region. When it comes to 'inevitable' criminal activities zones securitization is not enough to contain crime. Furthermore, sometimes 'inevitable' criminal activities can be necessary as they may act as a bridge for the transition to the new economic reality in the countries of SEE. In conclusion, law-abiding businessmen need to be facilitated as much as possible so that they will not resort to criminal activities.

- In order to successfully fight organized crime we need to know more details about how criminal networks operate. However, it is hard to find such information and it is dangerous to undertake field-research in this area. Even when information is available it is very hard to find evidence that can be accepted in court. In this context one should be careful with the data that are available as often it is leaked to the media by members of the intelligence services which are themselves partially involved in criminal activities.

- It is important to determine what knowledge is currently most essential in the fight against organized crime and whether it is available or not. If it is not available resources and energy need to be allocated to this end.

- It is due to links between political, financial and criminal interests in the countries of SEE that the fight against organized crime is so difficult. The fact that police enforcement agents as well as judges are heavily politicized and therefore are in the service of politicians and not of the state greatly undermines efforts to stamp out crime. It is essential for the international community to think of ways to break this nexus down.

- When it comes to policing in the countries of SEE there is no effective system of providing a quick and effective response to citizens who have fallen victim to criminal activities or to those who wish to report criminal activities.

- It is accepted that the fight against organized crime to a large extent depends on institutional and legal reforms. In order to achieve such reforms in SEE two things are primarily required: (a) the ruling elites (who are at times entangled in criminal activities themselves) need to have an incentive to promote reform; (b) those social forces which are in favour of combating organized crime need to be mobilized. Therefore, the international community needs to present the regional elites with incentives and the society with realistic means which will facilitate social mobilization in the battle against crime.

- It is an often-repeated observation that weak states in SEE are one of the causes for the expansion of crime in the region. It is worth considering whether this is entirely true. States in the Balkans are strong in terms of expenditure, they run complex centralized systems, maintain controls over borders and assume many functions which should not be in state hands. All that activity takes place in a heavily bureaucratized environment. This state of affairs gives state officials power which in its turn more often than not breeds corruption and fosters close links between crime and the state. To break down this nexus the answer may be found perhaps in the question 'what can the state do less?' In other words, the controlling role of the state should be diminished and the state should derive its power from enforcing the law. Criminal networks are essentially economic enterprises based on the supply and demand rules of the market, but operating outside the law. Therefore, the best means to combat them may not be with more state controls but through the development of strong market forces which operate within the law.

- The history of crime shows that it reaches a point when it wishes for its activities to become legitimate. Therefore we need to think how criminals can be enticed to make the break into legitimacy.
- There has to be a better understanding of the needs on the ground of law enforcement officers, particularly when it comes to their need for protection.
- Since there are close links between criminal networks in western Europe and SEE it is important for western Europe to examine what it can be done to this end to weaken/destroy these links.
- The international community often indirectly supports crime through its links and support for corrupt governments in SEE when these are co-operating with the international community on certain special issues.
- There is not enough cooperation/coordination and information sharing against transborder organized crime at a regional level in SEE. More specifically, in the law enforcement community individuals know one another well and work well together; the problem starts when we move to a more senior level and particularly when the judiciary takes over.
- International institutional cooperation against organized crime works well in theory but not in practice. Essentially there is no effective sharing of information. On the other hand, as it is well known, there is a lot of overlap, with the result that resources are stretched thin. We need to bridge the gap between theory and practice when it comes to the question of international institutions' cooperation.
- There is lack of real proposals from international organizations, the EU and governments in SEE as to what needs to be done on the ground. There are statements but what is needed is coordinated action and budgets to support them.

- Recently there has been an effort to build a consensus regarding priorities and strategies in dealing with organized crime among international institutions. Nonetheless, as the political will rests with national governments this act demands a lot of diplomacy and it has been proven not to be easy.
- It is only a matter of time before crime will move to a more sophisticated phase assisted by cutting-edge information technology. However, there is still no real thinking or cooperation of policy in view of such a threat.
- Organized crime has global networks and global impact. In this context it is worth keeping in mind that there are links between crime and international terrorism.
- The delay in determining the legal status of Kosovo only helps to boost organized crime there.

Policy Recommendations

- The right balance between prevention and law enforcement should be found in order to succeed in the battle against organized crime.
- It is important to de-criminalize activities which fall into the realm of 'inevitable' crime resulting from inadequate or outdated laws and regulations.
- It is important to inform and educate the public in SEE as to what constitutes crime and its medium- and long-term negative consequences. In this effort we have to win the battle for capturing the hearts and minds of youth. To this end the international community needs to commit financial resources which among other things should provide serious job opportunities to the young.
- Normally there are no arrests of the big crime bosses but of the middle- and lower-level actors. There has to be intensive publicity about known crime leaders as it helps to sensitize the public as well as increase pressure on the elites to act.
- In the context of policing there is an urgent need to establish an anti-crime help-line in the states of SEE, to facilitate citizens and foreign visitors to report criminal activities and to assist them when they fall victims of crime.
- As a step in the direction of breaking links between political, financial and criminal interests the reform of party financing in SEE states is essential. Party financing needs to be regulated and parties have to account for their financial resources.
- There has to be coordinated activity against organized crime both at a regional and international level.

- Strong attention should be given and preemptive action should be taken both at a national and at a transnational level against the imminent threat of marriage between criminal activities and high-tech.
- It is generally accepted that 'following the money' is a sure way of cracking down criminal networks. The introduction of internationally accepted procedures which would allow swift and effective cooperation between countries to this effect is therefore essential. Crime money which has been confiscated should be used to finance anti-crime activities.
- Governments should be held accountable for failing to effectively deal with crime. To this effect the answer may be the establishment of an International Court for crimes against international society which will have the power to indict politicians or other citizens who show no real interest in fighting against crime.
- The EU should develop and implement a long-term policy of integration of the western Balkans into Europe, particularly in the area of justice/public order and immigration.
- As a means of achieving the reduction of organized crime the EU and the countries of SEE should develop mutually fruitful cooperation through the establishment of a regime of short-term work permits in countries of the EU for SEE citizens. This regime should have to be closely monitored to avoid the abuses of SEE temporary workers by their EU employers or the immigration of 'unsuitable' elements to the EU. To this effect it is important to improve the quality of SEE passports so that they cannot be easily falsified as is currently the case. Particular emphasis has to be given to increasing the accessibility of the EU labour market for women from SEE, as that perhaps would obviously have the most direct impact on reducing organized crime, since after drugs trafficking, human trafficking is the second most profitable illegal activity. In the same direction EU governments could allow SEE citizens to establish self-employed businesses in sectors which suffer a serious shortage of EU skills.
- When it comes to the area of border policing many EU states are porous. There is a need for a better-trained and stronger EU police force which should also be involved in policing the inter-Balkan state borders. In this context the EU could perhaps follow examples from the US experience in policing its Latin American border.
- As a step in the direction of enhancing regional transborder cooperation against organized crime, regular senior level meetings for discussion of methods, coordination of action and exchange of information at a regional level need to be introduced with the participation of EU officials.

- It is imperative that legal structures across the countries in SEE and western Europe are standardized.
- It is imperative that a system of thorough training and control of all foreign forces based in SEE be put in place so as to ensure that their personnel do not get involved in criminal activities.

NOTE

1. Organized by the Hellenic Foundation for European and Foreign Policy (ELIAMEP) in cooperation with the Center for Liberal Strategies, Sofia; with the support of the German Marshall Fund of the United States and the Open Society Foundation, Sofia.

ELIAMEP's Forum on New Security Issues (FONSI): 'Shared Interests & Values between Southeastern Europe & The Transatlantic Community'

WORKSHOP ON 'PERCEPTIONS REGARDING ORGANIZED CRIME IN SOUTHEASTERN EUROPE: IS THERE AN INFORMATION GAP?', 24–26 JUNE 2003, ATHENS[1]

EXECUTIVE SUMMARY

Rapporteur: Ekavi Athanassopoulou

Public Perceptions

The public in the countries of southeast Europe (SEE) is for the most part only generally informed about organized crime and not of its implications and/or the extent of its activities. Organized crime is not addressed by the media as a well-established line of business. What normally attracts a short span of attention from the media are big scandals. Detailed information and in-depth analysis which can fuel serious public interest and awareness of the long-term dangers and negative repercussions that organized crime has for the economy, the political life and society of the country are lacking.

The public in SEE, being aware of state corruption which feeds on criminal activities, shows more and more apathy regarding organized crime, as it believes that since the state does not fight against organized crime there is nothing else that can be done.

On the other hand, a great part of the public in SEE considers organized crime an attractive byproduct of capitalism as it generates income in otherwise slow-growing or stagnant economies. The fact that to a large extent criminal activities go unpunished as a result of state corruption enhances the attraction of crime to many citizens. There is also a very broad public consensus in the countries of SEE that success is pegged to criminality. In other words, the prevailing perception is that very little can be achieved without resort to illegal means.

Often the public perceives organized crime in its own country as an imported phenomenon, due to the way organized crime activities are portrayed by the domestic press; this perception often results in feelings of xenophobia.

The business community in SEE is much more aware of how organized crime works, as the monopolistic nature of organized crime activities and mafias' cooperation with the state destroy the free market and fair competition environment within which legal businesses are trying to operate. Some members of the business community in SEE point out that even when illegal businesses become legitimate they do not leave behind the illegal methods they were used to; thus, they still undermine free competition. Unfortunately the business communities in all SEE countries are not well organized to lead a public information campaign and galvanize a reaction against organized crime and crime-supporting state corruption.

The Role of the Media

The media in SEE are both part of the problem and the solution when it comes to successfully informing the public about organized crime.

More often than not the information provided by the media is limited, local in character and partial (depending on who their sponsor is the media focus attention on competitors to their sponsor criminals). Links between local criminals and groups in other countries are not explored; the focus is on the victims of criminal activities and not the criminals themselves and their wide supportive networks. To a large extent this is the result of the lack of financial independence of the media. The media in SEE in its fight for survival in a tight market are infiltrated by local mafia bosses who are emerging as media owners or sponsors.

Often governments in SEE (the example of the Romanian government was stressed in the workshop) put pressure against media reporting on big mafia activities in their countries, wishing to avoid blackening the image of the government both domestically and internationally.

In the multiethnic states of SEE the media of different ethnic communities find it often difficult to cooperate with each other in reporting on organized crime which cuts across ethnic divisions. Part of the problem is that their audiences finds it easier to criminalize in their minds members of the other ethnic communities.

In the final analysis the way that the media address organized crime reflects the fact that SEE societies are politicized and far from being information societies.

The Role of Civil Society

The public in SEE to a large extent believes that the fight against organized crime is a police problem; it does not see it also as a social problem.

Civil society cannot hope to achieve much against organized crime given the overwhelming scale of organized crime activities. Therefore, it has to chose its battles carefully and focus its efforts.

To this end NGOs in SEE can play a very important role in mobilizing civil reaction against organized crime as they are financed by foreign capital and therefore maintain their independence from criminal networks.

Organized crime thrives in societies where there is low social capital, i.e. citizens have little trust in each other. The countries of SEE fall into this category. Civil solidarity in SEE has been lost as a result of the tremendous political, economic and social change the post-Communist countries have gone through.

The Role of Governments

Governments in SEE do not generally include in their policies against organized crime the need to sensitize the public regarding organized crime activities. Very often governments find it difficult to take on the political cost of systematically stamp out illegal activities as these offer income to a number of families in their countries.

THE BATTLE AGAINST ORGANIZED CRIME: CONCLUSIONS AND RECOMMENDATIONS

- Organized crime is the result of confluence of at least the following factors: transition to democracy, transition to a free market, low income levels and income inequality. It is essential to acquire more information and analysis regarding organized crime in order to be more able to fight against it. Transnational data on organized crime in particular are missing.
- Academic research has to try to be more in touch with Western policy makers and their priorities in addressing the problem of organized crime in SEE, so as to have major practical impact.
- The strategy against organized crime in SEE has to be redrawn as we are faced with the phenomenon of alliances between mafia and state.
- The lack of the rule of law and of properly working institutions in SEE is a fundamental handicap in the fight against crime.
- Campaigns against organized crime should be substituted by campaigns in favour of reforming and strengthening public institutions. At the

same time it has to be kept in mind that policing is not enough and economic development policies need also to be employed.

- So far there has been no true political will in the countries of SEE to address the need for legal institutional reforms which will facilitate the battle against organized crime. It is in the interest of the international community to employ a carrot-and-stick policy so as to ensure that, first, SEE governments change their 'soft' perceptions regarding organized crime and corruption in their countries, and second, they seriously commit themselves to the necessary reforms and to the fight against organized crime. International organizations have to work harder themselves and think in more depth in order to successfully address the challenges they are faced with in SEE.

- With particular reference to the EU, Brussels has proved to be an extremely weak player in pressing the necessity of judicial reform on SEE governments. The Copenhagen criteria should include more requirements when it comes to the chapter on home and justice affairs.

- The international community should take the initiative and bear pressure upon SEE governments to increase transnational intelligence, police and judicial cooperation.

- At a more practical level there is an absolute need for the countries of SEE to introduce modern methods of fighting organized crime, including the use of modern technology.

ENHANCING PUBLIC AWARENSS OF THE NEGATIVE EFFECTS OF ORGANIZED CRIME: CONCLUSIONS AND RECOMMENDATIONS

- There is a strong need for more research on the relationship between public perceptions regarding organized crime and the growth of organized crime in SEE.

- Pressure from the EU and the international community on the governments in SEE to seriously deal with organized crime has proven not to be enough. Unless there is strong public pressure to make the state attack organized crime the battle against crime cannot be won. Therefore there is an absolute necessity to find means to educate the public regarding the ruinous long-term effects of organized crime and mobilize it against it. In many SEE countries the media has a negative image as it is seen as part of the political game which the public views negatively. Therefore, it is not perhaps in the strongest position to inspire the public in a campaign against organized crime. Nonetheless, the media and civil society NGOs have to find ways to make the public truly aware of the degree of organized crime activities in their countries and to shake off public apathy. The NGOs in particular have to seek ways to contribute to restoration of sense of civility among the public.

- In the fight against organized crime international cooperation between media, civil society NGOs and business is essential, as organized crime is not a local but a transnational phenomenon.
- With particular reference to the role of the media, investigating reporting on organized crime can be strengthened through transnational cooperation. In other words, reporting should take place in parallel in many countries, so as to achieve a major impact on the public mind, by showing the transnational nature of organized crime.
- The creation of international organized crime investigation reporting teams offers also the advantage that reporters can overcome problems of intimidation they are faced with when they investigate crime in their own countries.
- Visa requirements for journalists from SEE who wish to travel abroad as part of their investigation of organized crime should be eased.
- Laws regarding ownership transparency and funding of the media have to be enacted and strictly enforced.
- Laws which facilitate the investigation of organized crime should be put in place and enforced.
- So far the international community has given money to the media in SEE for training purposes. Though this kind of funding has been essential international sponsors today should support projects which aim at a serious investigative reporting of organized crime in SEE and at international networking among investigating reporters.

NOTE

1. Organized by the Hellenic Foundation for European and Foreign Policy (ELIAMEP); with the support of the German Marshall Fund of the United States.

INDEX

9 780415 348 01